THE SOCIAL WORK
Practicum

AN ACCESS GUIDE

SECOND EDITION

BARBARA THOMLISON
GAYLA ROGERS
DONALD COLLINS
RICHARD M. GRINNELL, JR.

Faculty of Social Work
The University of Calgary

F.E. Peacock Publishers, Inc. ■ Itasca, Illinois 60143

DEDICATED TO ALL social work practicum instructors,
practicum liaisons, practicum tutorial teachers,
practicum directors, and their students

Contents

Foreword

THE PRACTICUM IN SOCIAL WORK education is clearly focused on teaching students how to help others help themselves with "real life problems"—the mission of social work. The practicum also takes on a "larger than life" significance in the professional development of our students as well. Perhaps it is because the practicum is the place where students actually learn how to do something of concrete value with others. Or, maybe it is because their "doing" is so closely tied to their "knowing," which is closely tied to their "becoming professionals who can be trusted and committed to the well-being of others."

For such reasons, the practicum learning experience has a great appeal for our students, our faculty, and our profession alike. Without a doubt, it is the primary means by which we prepare the next generation of social workers who will engage and assist people who live in a complicated, ever-changing, and problematic world. This is easier said than done, however, considering the multiple objectives of the practicum: to teach skills and values that must be integrated with the students' classroom learning and life experiences all within a practicum setting. Across North America and Britain, there is a resurgence of critical attention and scholarship in the content and educational processes of the social work practicum. This book clearly contributes to this important tide and is especially meaningful since it is centered on the students' past and present life, work, and learning experiences.

The authors have diligently yet lightly presented the essential components for a social work student to have a successful practicum. By defining the salient elements and players, and describing the "practicum process" over time, the authors skillfully provide a very practical and informative guide. To seize upon the journey metaphor used throughout the book, most of us need guides, guidelines, and signposts to chart our voyages, to have some sense of where we are bound, and to appreciate our individual journies. The experienced traveler knows firsthand that we can never fully anticipate what will happen or how we will change when embarking on a journey into uncharted territory.

Truly, a major part of the adventure is encountering the unexpected revelations of self and human dilemmas. Nonetheless, we would be foolish not to take into account our personal resources, our intentions, and the resources that are available within our faculty and community so we can launch rather than lurch into the practicum. This book pays proper attention to the coordination of the primary constituencies of the social work practicum which include: field agencies, their programs, and service missions; client populations; practicum faculty; learning expectations of the social work program; and the students as colleagues and consumers. These various groups prepare the ship for castoff. The book then presents the process of the total student learning experience by moving from the social work student as student-observer to student-participant to student-practitioner with increasing autonomy, skill, and self-confidence—the essence of the voyage as charted throughout the book.

Students using the supportive exercises contained at the end of each chapter (as well as the two appendices) will help establish an environment conducive to student learning and will avoid unnecessary diversions. In a similar vein, most of us have found that problems in practicums stem, in a large part, from students, practicum instructors, practicum liaisons, and practicum tutorial teachers either not understanding their respective responsibilities or not following through competently or completely. This book maintains that not knowing one's role (and cutting corners) undercuts the necessary foundation for a student to have a meaningful practicum learning experience.

As we all know too well, a social work student can merely survive a practicum and "get through to the end," but there is always something lost when this happens. On balance, it is important to recognize that proper planning and preparation alone will not assure a student's success.

Considerable effort and hard work, responsiveness to criticism, and, of course, some talent, motivation, and commitment are necessary to bring our students to the destination of their choice.

We are all traveling companions along the journey contained in this book. The journey through time is marked by noting that the practicum within social work education is in its centennial decade. For a hundred years, more or less, social work students have been learning their craft and their profession "out in the field" under the expert guidance of seasoned and competent practitioners. Through a century of unparalleled change, social work students have been challenged, sometimes frustrated, and inspired by the social problems faced by many people.

The book asserts that a student's journey begins but does not really end with the conclusion of the practicum. Rather the journey continues throughout a student's career of change, struggle, and achievement. In an ideal sense, the authors maintain that we can never be a finished product. Rather, we should always be striving for deeper understandings, firmer resolve, and more effective skills through reflection and disciplined effort.

The practicum should provide the opportunity for developing the essential habits of mind—the spirit and the character that will substain our students' efforts through a lifetime of service to others and society. The wisdom and perspective contained in this book can go a long way to ensure the integrity and the quality of the social work practicum. And realizing this vital goal will ultimately sustain and advance contemporary social work practice.

Dean Schneck
School of Social Work
University of Wisconsin at Madison

*I wish I knew what I was getting into
when I signed up for my first practicum.*
— A Student

Preface for Students

W E HAVE WRITTEN THIS BOOK for you, a social work student who is about to go on a practicum journey for the first time. We believe your trip will be more successful if you follow our guided tour as laid out within the pages that follow. Like other travel guides, ours provides you with routes, overviews of what to expect, suggestions of what to see and where to stop along the way, some detailed road maps, explanations of important landmarks, and how to react when you have made the wrong turn or the unexpected happens.

Your practicum journey will take you on a route specifically designed for you. Even though your trip will be an individualized one, you will also have travel guides who will accompany you on your trip. In addition to our book, you will also have others who will help you as you embark on your practicum experience:

✔ You will have your own two personalized tour guides to help you on your journey—your practicum instructor and practicum liaison.

✔ You will have a group guide who will group-instruct you and your classmates who are taking similar routes—your practicum tutorial teacher.

✔ Your practicum journey will have a tour organizer to ensure that everyone's journey has the ingredients for being successful—your program's practicum director.

✔ Finally, you may have a companion traveler(s) who will accompany you on your trip—one or two of your classmates may share the same practicum setting as you.

With all of these people involved in your practicum experience, you should feel confident embarking on your journey, even though you may be entering new territory and covering ground you have never seen before. Thus, your trip will not be a solo one.

PURPOSE AND GOALS

We have departed from the conventional book format in ways that we believe will reduce any practicum-induced anxieties that you may have. Our purpose is for you to have a satisfying, challenging, and productive learning exchange throughout your entire practicum journey. Keep our purpose in mind while reviewing our three simple goals:

✔ to ensure that your practicum is a *learning* experience and not a *working* experience.

✔ to link your classroom learning with your practicum learning.

✔ to promote the partnerships (e.g., your practicum instructor, your practicum liaison, your practicum tutorial teacher, your practicum director, and your classmates) involved in your practicum learning.

In short, our aim is to assist you in navigating the various bi-ways and highways on the way to becoming a competent social worker—to take over the wheel for the first time, by providing you with a taste of what it might be like to drive on your own.

There are, however, three noteworthy goals that our book does *not* attempt to accomplish. First, the ideas, procedures, and suggestions contained here are not intended as a substitute for your program's practicum manual and handouts. Second, the book does not teach practice skills. Many other books teach them with a depth and breadth that we could not hope to duplicate in this small volume. Finally, we do not provide an exhaustive array of practice theories to cover every unique practicum situation.

WHEN AND HOW TO USE OUR BOOK

The Social Work Practicum is designed to approximate the progression of phases as your practicum unfolds. We present a summary of what you should expect along the way as you plot your personal learning path. You can use this book in three ways, depending on the kind of traveler you are:

✔ If you are the kind of traveler who wants to know everything that could happen and all about what you are going to see before you even leave home, then you can read the entire book in advance of your journey.

✔ If you are the kind of traveler who cannot really absorb the details until just before you arrive at a particular point along the way, then you can read specific sections as they become applicable to your unique situation.

✔ On the other hand, if you have never found guidebooks particularly helpful in general, you have likely found them useful as a resource to turn to when you cannot find the information anywhere else. If this is the case, our book is designed so you can refer to only parts of it as your needs arise.

In summary, unlike many others, this book does not have to be read sequentially. You can open to any chapter and read forward or backward. How you use our book also depends on the way your program offers its practicum. Some programs offer practicums through a block placement format, while others prefer a concurrent arrangement. Some students, therefore, are taking social work classroom courses at the same time they are in their practicums, whereas others have completed most of their courses prior to their practicums.

As a consequence, many students are at different phases of their total social work learning experiences when they enter their practicums. In addition, some students make rapid progress through the learning phases while others move more slowly. Our book provides you with the opportunity to progress at your own pace by completing the exercises as they become applicable.

Exercises and Activities

We have included exercises and activities at the end of each chapter to assist you in the art of making sure that your activities result in a practicum in which you learn useful material that you can apply in actual practice situations; exercises and activities also ensure that what you learn from specific situations can be transferred to other social work contexts. They are designed to help you make sense of your experiences and to link what you are reading, discussing, and thinking about with what you are doing.

The exercises are presented with "Notes on Use" to guide you, your practicum instructor, and your practicum tutorial teacher in how to use them in various contexts. Each exercise is described according to its type and purpose. Some are for self-study and some are to be used with other exercises. Some are used to *explore* an issue, theme, or aspect of practice; others are there to help you *reflect* on a practice element; others are *applications* of practice; while still others combine elements.

ORGANIZATION

With these purposes and goals in mind, we have organized *The Social Work Practicum* to suit individual social work programs and individual student learning needs. To do this we have divided the text into four parts. Each part deals with a different aspect of your practicum journey.

✔ Part One is like a travelogue. It tells you a little bit about your destination and some of the things you might encounter along the way. There are two chapters to help you understand why you are taking this trip in the first place and what you can expect. It also covers what you are bringing on your journey so that you are fully aware of the strengths you possess and how you can use these strengths to help you in areas that challenge you.

✔ Part Two takes you from your last-minute preparations to the first few weeks of your journey. Planning is key to managing the uncertainties and unknowns involved in getting started. This is about orienting yourself and getting specific about mapping out the details of your journey. The two chapters in this section are designed to help you chart the path for your unique route.

✔ Part Three contains three chapters that might be analogous to detailed road maps. Each one will help you navigate a different part of your journey. One will assist you on the path you take with your practicum instructor. The next will direct you through the details of making sense of your day-to-day activities. The third will help you to evaluate your chosen path as you go, so that you can make changes to your itinerary while you are en route.

✔ Part Four has two chapters. One is designed to help you deal with the unexpected that occurs along the way. It may be that bad weather ahead has forced a route change, it may be that you took a wrong turn and you need to backtrack a bit, or you may find that you are on the wrong road altogether. Whatever the case, this part outlines some of the unexpected events that may occur. The final chapter prepares you for your journey's end and begins your thinking about your next trip. If you are not going into another practicum setting, you can use this part to begin to prepare for job-related activities.

✔ Finally, the book contains two appendixes that will be useful to you as you go through your practicum. The first appendix is the NASW's *Code of Ethics*, which will be instrumental to you throughout your entire social work career. You will need it as you formulate your learning goals and objectives while you are in your practicum, and the *Code* will guide your ethical obligations as you strive to become a professional social worker. The second appendix is an example of a generic mid-term and final evaluation form.

KEEPING YOUR TRIP TOGETHER

We recommend that you purchase a three-ring binder for your practicum course. These pages are three-hole punched and perforated for that purpose. Your program's practicum manual and practicum handouts can also be added to your binder so a complete guide to your practicum educational experience is then self-contained and individualized for you. The perforated pages allow you to hand in completed exercises to your practicum instructor, your practicum tutorial teacher, or your practicum liaison, or to share them with your classmates.

As with the first edition, we had a good time writing the second. We used first and last names within the text to add a bit of pizazz; however, the names, characters, places, and incidents within our book are either the product of the authors' imaginations or are used fictitiously. In the interest of simplifying pronouns, we chose to use the female form with the clear understanding that the words "she" and "her" include "he" and "his." Any resemblance to actual events, locales, or persons (living or dead) is entirely coincidental. We hope that the apparent levity with which we have treated the practicum will be accepted in the same spirit as it is meant. Our intention is not to diminish the practicum experience; rather, it is to present it with humor, warmth, and humanness so that your first contact with it will be a positive one.

WHAT'S NEW IN THIS EDITION?

We listened closely to the feedback given to us by the students, practicum instructors, and practicum tutorial teachers who used the first edition. In doing so, we have retained, thrown out, and added content to improve the quality and overall utility of the book. We added, eliminated, refined, and reworked many of the exercises. We added "Notes for Use" for you, your practicum instructor, and your practicum tutorial teacher in an effort to use the exercises more effectively. In terms of the content, we have included more on practicum theory and processes of learning and on cultural diversity issues within practicum settings.

As we have previously mentioned, although *The Social Work Practicum* is written directly for you, your practicum instructor, your practicum liaison, and your practicum tutorial teacher may also find this edition more useful to them as a reference and source book since it contains more practicum learning theory, better self-study exercises, and many more interactive activities and practicum tutorial seminar tasks.

ACKNOWLEDGMENTS

The four of us have been practicum instructors, practicum liaisons, practicum directors, practicum tutorial teachers, and practice methods teachers for longer than we wish to recall. We thank the countless number of social work students whom we had the privilege of teaching and learning from, as they have directly contributed to the conceptual mapping and development of this book.

Within the limits of strict time frames and resources, we have strived to follow the suggestions offered by our colleagues; however, they should not be held responsible for our sins of omission or commission. We wish to express our appreciation to Doreen Neville for her help in the preparation of the final manuscript. We also wish to fondly remember Marj Andrukow, whose contribution was invaluable. We extend our sincere appreciation to Ray J. Thomlison, our Dean, who provided the necessary academic milieu and encouragement to help us see the book to completion.

We would be remiss not to mention that the friendly folks at F. E. Peacock Publishers have been more than supportive in our adventure into uncharted territory, and it is a privilege to publish once again under the Peacock banner.

YOU CAN NEVER GET LOST ON
THE ROAD TO INTEREST

We hope this second edition will be of use to you in your journey into the uncharted territory of your practicum. In this spirit, we offer our book to you—the future social work practitioner. We hope you will keep it on your bookshelf and refer to it from time to time. If *The Social Work Practicum* helps you to expand your practicum-related knowledge and skills in becoming more effective with your future clients, our efforts will have been more than justified. If it also encourages you to become a practicum instructor in order to continue the pursuit of a coherent practical base for social work practice, our task will be fully rewarded. ☺

January 1996   *Barbara Thomlison*
Gayla Rogers
Donald Collins
Richard M. Grinnell, Jr.

THE SOCIAL WORK
Practicum

AN ACCESS GUIDE

SECOND EDITION

Part One

Let Your Journey Begin

THE TWO CHAPTERS OF PART ONE form a beginning travelogue for your journey into your first practicum experience. They provide you with a bit of information about your destination and detail some of the things you might encounter at the beginning of your trip. Taken together, the two chapters should help you to understand why you are taking this trip in the first place and what you can expect.

Part One will help you become aware of some of the strengths and weaknesses that you will be bringing on your journey. Knowing your strengths and weaknesses will prepare you for the challenges that you will experience toward your destination and goal—becoming a competent social worker.

Chapter One

The anxiety and stress about what is to
come is worse than actually doing it!
— A Student

Your Journey in Context

C LIENTS SEEKING YOUR HELP to solve their problems are not much interested if you can write a brilliant treatise on "problem solving." Neither are they interested in the grade you received for your last practice methods paper. Clients are consumers of your service and they just want *you* to do *it*—just as when you take your car into the shop to be fixed by a mechanic. Like you with the mechanic, clients want you to get on with doing *it*, in a very practical way. If possible, they want you to have done *it*, or something like *it* before.

The point of a *social work practicum* is to learn how to do *it* and what it means to do *it* well: how to apply theoretical social work knowledge within hands-on situations; how to cope with the practical limitations of real-life social service environments; what it means to be useful to real people with real problems in real social work settings that are sometimes unpredictable and less than "ideal." For you and all future social workers, the importance of knowing and understanding how to help people and then actually doing *it* competently cannot be overstated.

Knowing, thinking, being, and doing start to come together in your first practicum experience. By now you should have had plenty of opportunity to show what you *know* and how you *think* through your term papers, exams, and other classroom-based assignments. You may have had some opportunities to practice *being* and *doing* in your communication labs or role plays in some of your courses. These activities may prepare you for the real world of practice but they are not substitutes for the "real thing." This is why the "practicum portion" of learning how to do social work is such an important part of your "total social work program." First you need to know what a practicum is, and what it is not. Armed with this knowledge, you can then appreciate how it fits into the whole of your total social work educational experience as you embark upon your journey toward becoming a competent practitioner.

You may want to think of your practicum experience as a significant side trip along your learning journey. This journey, like others you have taken during your lifetime, will change you in various ways. And the practicum portion of your journey, especially your first practicum, will likely be the instigator of many of those changes.

Because of the nature of the learning that occurs throughout, your practicum experience will have a long-lasting impact on you. There is something about being in a place where real social work is done by real social workers; having some responsibility for actually doing social work yourself; knowing something about the problems, issues, or concerns addressed through social work services; understanding how social work processes produce change; and lastly, forming a relationship with your practicum instructor that accelerates your learning, growth, development, and change. All these experiences can be both very exhilarating and threatening at the same time.

YOUR PRACTICUM IS ...

Your practicum is a required core course in your social work program. Accredited social work programs require that students spend a minimum number of hours in real-life practice settings, supervised by qualified practicum instructors; many programs require more than the minimum, however. Your practicum(s) can range from one-quarter to one-third of your total social work educational experience.

Depending on your particular program, you may have two or more distinct practicum courses and/or practicum settings. Social work programs vary in the format that their practicums can take, the places where "social work" is done, the way in which the practicum process is administered, and the phases in which the practicum unfolds. The most important thing to remember at this point is that practicum formats vary as much as social work programs. Let us now turn to the different formats that practicums can take.

Practicum Formats

Your practicum may be taken as a block placement, in which you go to your practicum setting full time for a term, quarter, or semester. During a block placement, you may take only a practice methods course or a practicum tutorial course (to be discussed shortly). A second possibility is that you may take your practicum in a concurrent format. This means that you go to your practicum setting for part of the week and continue to take classroom courses—such as human behavior, research, social policy, interviewing, electives, and so forth—during the other part of the week. Generally speaking, both practicum formats provide you with the same total number of hours in your practicum setting.

Preference for one format has nothing to do with hours; rather, it is concerned with the advantages and disadvantages of a total immersion in your practicum as compared with a part-classroom, part-practicum setting format. For example, a student who exists half in school and half in a practicum setting (not to mention the "third half" which goes home occasionally) might feel torn between the demands of classroom course work and the demands of the practicum setting. It might be tempting to skip class to accommodate a new client or to spend the day reading to finish a term paper. On the other hand, you might find it easier to integrate your practicum experience with your classroom courses when both are occurring simultaneously. If you are taking a class on group work, for example, it might be helpful if your practicum setting does group work of some kind.

Practicum Tutorials

As we mentioned earlier, some social work programs use the block practicum format and others use a concurrent format. Some programs use one format for the undergraduate program and the other for the graduate program. Most tailor the format to the needs and resources of the local social service agencies that are affiliated with the social work program. A majority of social work programs ensure that practicum and classroom courses are integrated by providing practicum tutorials that are sometimes called *integrative practice seminars* or *field seminars*.

Your practicum tutorial will help you to build theory from practice, apply theory to practice, and transfer and generalize your learning through exploration, reflection, and application. Your tutorial may be taught by your practicum liaison, your practicum instructor, or one of the instructors in your social work program. It may take place on your campus or right at your practicum setting, but its purpose is always the same: to help you to make sense of what you are experiencing, to integrate practice issues with theory, and to become an effective social work practitioner. Its main purpose is to integrate practice issues with practice theory by allowing you to discuss your practice experiences with your classmates. Preparation in the form of reading, reflection, and discussion is critical to achieving integration within this very important course.

Practicum Settings

As you know from your classroom courses, social workers function in many different settings. Some work only with individuals who have problems in a specific area, such as substance abuse, parenting, homelessness, or having too intimate an acquaintanceship with the criminal justice system. Some social workers work with groups, such as in anger management, self-help, and with foster parents. Some work with families, such as in family support or family preservation programs. Some social workers work with communities, such as welfare reform, community relations networks, and advocacy groups. Some work with organizations, such as coalitions of agencies, or interdisciplinary collaboration in service delivery. Some do research and some write books. Some social workers do all of the above, and some may specialize in one particular area.

We work in environments that range from our own offices, to small two-person agencies, to business offices, to large and complex bureaucracies and organizations, hospitals, schools, courts, neighborhoods, and many other places. We are known as social workers, probation officers, counselors, clinical social workers, family therapists, group workers, street workers, community workers, researchers, program planners, and policy analysts. Thus, practicum settings can take on a wide variety of contexts. Your actual setting may be a community, a social service agency or organization within a community, a program or department within an agency or organization, or a project within a program or department.

Practicum Processes

Most social work programs have offices where everything to do with practicums is administered and managed. Depending on the size of an individual program, an office can be staffed by several persons and a hive of humming computers or it may be a single person, working in a small area. Regardless of its size, there are many key people involved in the administration and delivery of your program's practicum, but none more key than the *practicum director*—sometimes called a *field director, practicum coordinator*, or *field coordinator*.

It is the task of the practicum director to ensure that there are enough practicum settings to accommodate all of the social work students, that the practicum settings are sufficiently varied to afford a meaningful choice, and that each practicum setting provides a real *learning* experience. As you know, social work is a large and diverse field. Because of this, the choice of potential practicum settings may be enormous and potentially confusing. The practicum director will select reputable practicum settings whose social work staff have the time, the interest, the knowledge, and the skills to provide you with good practice learning environments.

Generally speaking, the practicum director disseminates information to you about the available practicum settings within your local community. Each social work program has its own way of matching you with a practicum setting, a practicum instructor, and a practicum liaison. Even if you are initially disappointed, remember there are few (if any) perfect matches. Keeping an open mind can go a long way to making almost any student/setting/instructor/liaison match a valuable learning experience. And keep in mind that your social work program has previously screened out unsuitable practicum settings, instructors, and liaisons.

Practicum Phases

Your practicum experience will consist of phases, beginning with the process of matching you with a practicum setting. This involves your understanding the purpose and intent of a practicum setting within the context of your social work program. It includes learning about how you learn so that you can make the most out of your practicum experience. We will discuss all of this in Part One.

The second phase involves setting the itinerary, mapping out your expectations, stating your learning objectives, and specifying the tasks or activities available to help you achieve your learning objectives. It is all about getting started, getting to know your practicum instructor, and settling into your setting. It is also important at this stage that you and your practicum instructor create a meaningful learning environment. In part this entails trying to determine how you will know when you have learned what you set out to do. This usually comes together in the form of a learning agreement among you, your practicum instructor, and your practicum liaison. All of this will be presented in Part Two.

The third phase involves progressing and performing, carrying out the tasks and activities, participating in weekly supervision, and any other educational opportunities that are available to you. During this time you will likely be participating in a practicum tutorial, which we discussed earlier. All of these will help you transform what you are doing into meaningful learning and will help you examine and evaluate your work. This is all covered in Part Three.

Finally, your practicum journey will come to an end and you will spend some time summing it up, which is the fourth phase. It is important that you and your practicum instructor deal with any dilemmas or issues that result from leaving your clients and your practicum setting. It is also important for you to be clear about what you have learned and where you need to direct your energies so you can link this experience with what is to come next: perhaps another practicum setting or a job.

The emphasis on the evaluation of learning will differ in each social work program. Some programs require a formal mid-term evaluation of your progress during you practicum, while others do not. Some programs formally evaluate their practicum instructors, while others do not. In addition, some programs formally evaluate each practicum setting; and there are programs that do not view evaluation quite this formally. Above all, the evaluation of learning assists in providing a continuing quality practicum not only for you but for future practicum students as well. This is all covered in Part Four.

YOUR PRACTICUM IS NOT...

Since your social work program does not merely tell you "to find a job in the social work field and get some *practical* experience," your practicum is more than an apprenticeship. Instead, practicums are carefully designed to facilitate your learning in order for you to think and act as a professional social worker.

Apprentices learn by observing "masters" and copying what they see and hear. If your master is incompetent or has a few bad habits, chances are you will learn those as well. Also, you may not be able to recognize the incompetence because you have no alternative sources of information. Sometimes apprentices do not understand *why* they are doing *what* they are doing. They are simply trained to do a job, *not* to think about it. Social work has a different model. Our profession has combined learning from the experts and senior practitioners with teaching students to think critically about their own work, as well as the work they observe going on around them, and to make use of students' own strengths and abilities. With this information, you are able to see how the profession of social work fits into the larger picture.

Now that we know what a practicum is and what it is not, we will turn our attention to the complexities of the field.

OUR PROFESSION IS COMPLEX

The social work profession exists to provide humane and effective social services to individuals, families, groups, communities, and society so that people's social functioning may be enhanced and the quality of life improved. This is complex, multifaceted work and requires the ability to look both inside yourself and outside at the very structure of society—all at the same time.

This is indeed a challenge. Obviously, the enhancement of social functioning and the improvement of the quality of life are desirable goals. On the other hand, it is a comment on our society that the enhancing and improving needs to be done by *professionals*. What happened to Aunt Dorothy? To Grandpa? To the idea that if your roof leaks you repair it, if your fence falls down you rebuild it, and if your child has a problem you help solve it?

Like dentists and lawyers, social workers live in an age of specialization in which we categorize, subdivide, and do battle over respective turfs. Ms. Puccio's weak heart, for example, is looked at first by her family doctor, who then sends her to a cardiologist. Ms. Puccio's depression, helped along by the malfunctioning weak heart, falls to the social worker.

Ms. Puccio's elderly mother, whom she can no longer care for because she is depressed, is looked after by the gerontologist and the nursing home staff. Her children are taken into care by child welfare workers. Her husband, who has had an ongoing problem with alcohol, is being treated in a detoxification program.

Specializations

Specialization is not necessarily bad. Like everything else, it has its brighter and darker sides, and certainly Ms. Puccio, her husband, mother, and children have to be cared for somehow. The point is that specialization in social work may hold more potential dangers than specialization in other fields. If you hire a specialist to repair your roof, for example, you may be depriving yourself of the sense of accomplishment that comes from fixing it yourself. More likely, however, you will just be depriving yourself of the hours, the money, and, just maybe, a broken leg.

Hiring a specialist to mend your life is a different matter, however. Now you stand to lose such things as your sense of control, your self-esteem, and your confidence as a functioning and competent adult. Social work professionals are well aware of these dangers, and phrases such as "self-determination" and "helping others to help themselves" occur over and over again in social work books.

Your practicum experience is an opportunity to learn how to help. It is also an opportunity to learn when *not* to help—when *not* to take children out of their homes, when *not* to move Ms. Puccio's mother from her evil-smelling bedroom to a sterile-like nursing home, when *not* to take a juvenile back to court for breaking the terms of probation.

All of these "nots" involve ethical choices. For example, do you have the right to move Ms. Puccio's mother to "safety" against her wishes? Does your practicum setting have the right? Does our society have the right? Who makes these decisions?

On your journey through this book, these issues will become clearer in terms of how you, your practicum setting, and real-life practice dilemmas interface with one another.

YOUR PRACTICUM PATHWAY

There are various people who will be involved in your learning experience within your first practicum setting. These people are: your classmates, your program's practicum director, your practicum instructor, your practicum liaison, your practicum tutorial teacher, and yourself.

Your Classmates

You go to classes. You read books and articles. You are taught the knowledge and skills that you are supposed to apply in your practicum setting. In every good practicum experience there is a direct relationship between you, the experiences you will gain, and the knowledge you learn. The practice opportunities will be set at a level that you will find challenging but not overwhelming. And this is not as easy as it sounds because social work practice that is challenging to one student might be completely overwhelming to another, and downright boring to yet a third.

Look around at your classmates. A diverse group, they come from a variety of ethnic, racial, and cultural backgrounds. Some have recently graduated from high school. Some have worked in the social work profession for years and returned to school for a degree. Some may be physically challenged, some may have several orientations different from your own. Some are mature students with a great deal of life experience but no social work experience. Others are knowledgeable in one particular social work area but know little of other areas. You need to take all of these differences into account when planning your learning opportunities throughout your entire practicum experience.

As you can see, the practicum portion of learning social work is a specific type of educational journey. There are certain processes, roles, and responsibilities to be fulfilled so that your practicum experience will be effective. Each social work program may vary according to who performs the various practicum-related functions, but they all will occur.

Your Practicum Director

Your practicum director, like a tour organizer, is likely to be responsible for the overall coordination and administration of the practicum component of your social work program. The practicum director usually initiates the process of matching students with practicum settings, students with practicum instructors, students with practicum liaisons, and sometimes students with practicum tutorial teachers.

Your Practicum Instructor

Your practicum instructor, like a personal tour guide, shows you the way around. Practicum instructors are professional social workers usually employed by agencies where practicum settings are located. They communicate with your social work program via a practicum liaison. Often practicum instructors are responsible for assigning tasks and evaluating your progress and are responsible for the ongoing day-to-day instruction. You may, in fact, have more than one practicum instructor. It is important for you to remember that practicum instructors have a lot of competing demands on them.

First, practicum instructors must satisfy your social work program that its practicum standards are being met; second, they must match your skills, qualities, and potential with the services provided by the setting; third, they must protect the clients you will interact with from errors that could be made by beginning students; fourth, they endeavor to ensure smooth relationships between you and other staff within your practicum setting; and fifth, they must find the time to do all this.

Practicum instructors are in many ways the "heart of social work education."

Your Practicum Liaison

Your practicum liaison is usually a person from your social work program who is the link between your practicum instructor and your social work program. Often this person is responsible for your final grade (or pass/fail), via ongoing discussion with your practicum instructor. The practicum liaison is there to prevent or solve problems, enhance your learning, and support you and your practicum instructor when needed.

Your Practicum Tutorial Teacher

Your practicum tutorial teacher, also like a guide for a tour group, helps to integrate your practicum experience with the rest of the social work curriculum and your development as a professional in order to link all the pieces together. Sometimes these functions are separated, with the practicum liaison doing the linking and the practicum tutorial teacher doing the integration. Sometimes they are combined, with one person responsible for both functions.

You, the Student

The other important person in the journey involved in the communication, the bridge building, and the problem solving is *you*, the traveler in this journey. It is, after all, *your* learning experience, *your* future, the beginning of *your* professional life. It is your practicum experience, which you will never forget.

SUMMARY

We have provided you with a brief context for understanding the people, processes, and phases of your first practicum experience. We have used the metaphor of a journey to help you understand the intricacies and the uniqueness of your learning within your social work program. While we have attempted to present the commonalities across social work programs and processes, the journey is an individual one varying from student to student and from program to program.

Your practicum setting is an opportunity to apply theoretical knowledge to actual social work practice situations in a purposeful way. At one level, applying knowledge may involve remembering the theory behind engaging a client or terminating an interview. At a different level, applying knowledge means utilizing the total learning and understanding acquired throughout your lifetime in order to evaluate what you are doing, what your practicum setting is doing, and what the individual and societal consequences are likely to be. To do this effectively you need to know yourself, your values and assumptions, how you learn, when you learn most effectively, and what influences your responses to others. All of this background is what you pack and take with you on your journey.

Knowing what your practicum setting is doing is also an important part of fitting your own activities into the broader frame of our profession. Agencies and the practicum settings they contain—their types, goals, structures, and dynamics—will be discussed in Chapter Three. For now, it is enough to say that one of the goals of your practicum is to examine first your role within your practicum setting and its relationship within the social service delivery system and society in general. When you have done this, you will have a better understanding of whether you want to be a social worker, why you want to be a social worker, and what kind of social worker you want to be.

NOTES ON CHAPTER ONE:

Name: _____

EXERCISE 1.1: ASKING DIRECTIONS

Type: Exploration — Application

Purpose: To explore the various experiences of recent practicum students to find out firsthand what prospective practicum students need to bring or know before starting.

Exercise: Contact other social work students who have completed or are about to complete their practicums. Ask if there are things they know now that they wish they had known before they started. What advice, instructions, or directions can they provide you to help you focus on starting your practicum? Make a list of the topic questions you want to ask your classmates. Keep a list of what you want to remember. On the next page, write a summary of your discussions and insights you have gained from them.

Notes on Use

Student: This exercise is designed to give you information on how to ease your way into your practicum setting by exploring other students' experiences and applying what they learned to your preparations.

Practicum Instructor: Ask students what they learned by talking to other students who have just completed their practicums. Ask how that information might be useful to their individualized practicum setting. Explore with the students any unanswered questions. Offer your own suggestions.

Practicum Tutorial Teacher: Bring former practicum students into your class and have them briefly describe their practicum experiences and processes. Generate a list of things (on the following page) that students who have completed their practicums wish they had known before they started. Discuss ways to make use of this information so that your current students will be more prepared and feel less anxious about getting started.

✔ What former practicum students wish they had known before they began their practicums:

✔ Advice or suggestions from previous practicum students:

✔ Things I learned by asking questions:

Name: _____

EXERCISE 1.2: YOUR MIND MAP

_____

Type: Exploration — Reflection — Application

Purpose: To heighten your awareness of who you are and the influences on your life. To discover similarities and differences between and among students by sharing values, experiences, and influences.

Exercise: Make a map of values, experiences, and influences—such as family, school, religious, and others— that are important to you. On the following page, put a circle with your name in the center, then show lines extending from the center leading to information about you in various areas. After 30 minutes, show other students your mind map and then discuss your map with them.

Notes on Use

_____

Student: After drawing your mind map on the following page, reflect on the influences in your life including your background, family of origin, and any other interests that make you the person that you are. Share your map with the others by discussing your experiences. Compare the similarities and differences in your background, goals, and major experiences with those of other students.

Practicum Instructor and *Practicum Tutorial Teacher:* Ask students to draw a mind map of influences in their life, including background, family, and any experiences that have impacted them. Follow the student instructions for the drawing, then ask students to share their maps in small group formats. Questions for students can focus on the diversity and richness of their experiences, such as: What did you discover about the range of experiences and backgrounds of others? What do you know about the group now that you did not know before? Was it difficult to share your experiences? Was it difficult to chart your experiences? How would clients experience you?

✔ My personal mind map:

Name: _____

EXERCISE 1.3: PRACTICUM DESTINATIONS

Type: Reflection

Purpose: To consider your comfort level in working with different people with various problems in a variety of places.

Exercise: Social workers work with a variety of people in varying places with different types of problems, all requiring different helping processes. Some students find certain people or situations more or less challenging. How comfortable do you think you would feel working in some of the practicum settings that are listed on the following pages?

Notes on Use

Student: Working with the list of practicum settings starting on the following page, estimate a number that best reflects your comfort level. Rate each one on a five-point scale where 1 is "very uncomfortable" and 5 is "very comfortable." In the space provided below each setting, state your initial thoughts as to why you rated each setting as you did. Be candid in your responses and be prepared to share your list with others. Refer back to your mind map contained in Exercise 1.2. How do these influences affect your choices?

Practicum Instructor: Discuss your students' responses to this list. Ask your students about the influences that may have impacted their comfort levels in particular instances.

Practicum Tutorial Teacher: Have students discuss and compare with each other the range of responses and identify any misconceptions or misunderstandings about certain populations and the nature of social services to those populations.

1 = very uncomfortable ⇨ 5 = very comfortable

✔ A child abuse investigation program
   Rating_____
   Rationale:

✔ A needle exchange program
   Rating_____
   Rationale:

✔ An alcohol detoxification center
   Rating_____
   Rationale:

✔ A day hospital program for schizophrenics
   Rating_____
   Rationale:

✔ A neighborhood settlement house for immigrants
Rating_____
Rationale:

✔ A bereavement group for parents whose children are missing
Rating_____
Rationale:

✔ An inner-city shelter for the homeless
Rating_____
Rationale:

✔ A pro-choice counseling program
Rating_____
Rationale:

✔ A fund-raising program
Rating_____
Rationale:

✔ A hospice program for AIDS patients
Rating_____
Rationale:

✔ An advocacy rights group for gay/lesbian persons
Rating_____
Rationale:

✔ A training program for foster parents
Rating_____
Rationale:

✔ A suicide crisis line
  Rating_____
  Rationale:

✔ An inner-city high school
  Rating_____
  Rationale:

✔ A residential treatment program for adolescent sex offenders
  Rating_____
  Rationale:

✔ A work-for-welfare program for mothers
  Rating_____
  Rationale:

✔ An advocacy group for seniors
Rating_____
Rationale:

✔ A day care program for persons with Alzheimers
Rating_____
Rationale:

✔ A prison-based program for spouse abusers
Rating_____
Rationale:

✔ A program for violent adolescents
Rating_____
Rationale:

Name: _____

EXERCISE 1.4: YOUR POTENTIAL CONSUMER GROUP

Type: Reflection

Purpose: To consider the influences on your life, your comfort level with various client groups, and how this might affect your ability to work with diverse client problems.

Exercise: What client groups and problem areas suit you best? Make lists on the following two pages of client groups and problem areas you would and would not wish to work with. Consider your lists and try to attach a reason. Are there any client groups (e.g., frail elderly, abusive men, unemployed) or problem areas (e.g., substance abuse, homelessness, child sexual abuse) where you would rather *not* be placed? Make a list of these on the following pages.

Notes on Use

Student: Think about your past experiences with people who are different from you and how this might affect your ability to work with diverse groups. Reflect on your responses to the two lists you made and assess the possible implications for beginning your practicum.

Practicum Instructor: Ask students to explore what the two lists mean to them. Consider doing this exercise yourself and sharing it with your students, as well as, the ways in which you have addressed these issues.

Practicum Tutorial Teacher: Ask students to share with each other items from their two lists. Brainstorm strategies to address the implications for their ability to work effectively as a social worker when the two lists are compared with one another.

✔ Client groups I am comfortable with:

✔ Client groups I am not comfortable with:

✔ Problem areas I am comfortable dealing with:

✔ Problem areas I am not comfortable dealing with:

✔ Compare your four lists on the two previous pages and comment:

Name: _____

EXERCISE 1.5: TRAVEL INFORMATION

Type: Exploration

Purpose: To find the terms and definitions used by your practicum setting and your social work program to describe the key players and activities of your practicum experience.

Exercise: On the following pages you will find a list of the key terms and definitions used throughout this book. A definition is provided, but you need to write the terms and definitions that are used in your social work program. If the terms and definitions are the same, leave the spaces blank. Your terms and definitions are likely to be found in your program's practicum manual (if one is available). You can also get help from your practicum director, your practicum liaison, or your practicum tutorial teacher.

Notes on Use

Student: Every social work program has its own way of describing and defining the relevant practicum education terms. For this book, we have selected widely used terms and definitions, but it is important at the outset that you make certain you understand these terms in the context of your own social work program. That way, when these terms appear throughout this book, you can easily substitute words used by your program.

Practicum Instructor: Review the terms with your students. Point out any discrepancies and discuss fully. Identify any terms and definitions unique to your practice setting that are not included here.

Practicum Tutorial Teacher: Have students compare terms and discuss any discrepancies. Students can share which terms need clarifying with practicum instructors. Present any terms and definitions unique to your social program that are not included here.

✔ PRACTICUM: A required course in which you are enrolled. The practicum provides opportunities for you to apply the knowledge and skills learned in the classroom, especially from your practice methods course with different client systems. Also referred to as *field instruction* or *field work.*

Your Term and Definition:

✔ PRACTICUM DIRECTOR: Usually a faculty person who is responsible for developing, monitoring, and administering a wide range of practicum opportunities for students enrolled in the social work program. Also referred to as a *practicum coordinator, a field director,* or a *field coordinator.*

Your Term and Definition:

✔ PRACTICUM INSTRUCTOR: The social worker to whom you are assigned at your practicum setting. This person instructs, monitors, and usually evaluates the acquisition of your professional skills, knowledge, and values. This social worker is usually employed by the agency where your practicum setting is located. Also referred to as a *field supervisor* or a *field instructor.*

Your Term and Definition:

✔ PRACTICUM LIAISON: Usually a faculty-based person who is the link between your practicum instructor and your program's practicum director. This person is usually responsible for the assignment of your final grade based on discussions with your practicum instructor. Also referred to as a *field liaison*, a *practicum advisor*, or a *field advisor*.

Your Term and Definition:

✔ PRACTICUM MANUAL: The document that outlines the practicum educational process and requirements for social work students, practicum instructor, practicum liaisons, and the practicum director. Also referred to as a *practicum handbook* or a *field manual*.

Your Term and Definition:

✔ PRACTICUM SETTING: The place, agency, department, program, or project where your practicum is located and where you will actually do social work practice. Also referred to as a *field setting* or a *practicum placement*.

Your Term and Definition:

✔ PRACTICUM TUTORIAL: A required course that provides an opportunity for you to discuss your practicum issues and experiences and related classroom courses with other practicum students. Also referred to as a *field seminar* or an *integrative seminar*.

Your Term and Definition:

✔ PRACTICUM TUTORIAL TEACHER: The individual assigned to teach (lead or facilitate) the practicum tutorial. This person may be the practicum liaison, the practicum instructor, or a faculty instructor. Also referred to as a *tutorial leader* or a *seminar instructor*.

Your Term and Definition:

✔ SUPERVISORY CONFERENCE: Educationally focused supervisory meetings or conferences with you and your practicum instructor. They are usually held on a regular basis within your practicum setting. Educational supervision may be supplemented with group supervision or meetings with other staff and students. Also referred to as *supervisory sessions, field supervision, student supervision,* or *supervision conferences*.

Your Term and Definition:

Name: _____

EXERCISE 1.6: YOUR TRAVEL GUIDEBOOKS

Type: Reflection

Purpose: To gather meaningful and relevant information pertinent to the specific practice area, population, and program related to your practicum setting.

Exercise: Keep a record of what you read throughout your practicum experience. If you annotate the bibliography as you go, this compilation of sources will serve you for many years to come. Use the following headings to annotate what you read: Author, Title, Type of Article (e.g., research, conceptual, program description, narrative), Theme, and Key Findings. To begin, read three articles from professional social work journals about the population you will be working with in your practicum setting.

Notes on Use

Student: This exercise is an ongoing one throughout your practicum experience. It will enable you to build your knowledge base and keep track of all the information you have acquired. It will prove an invaluable resource to you in the future in working with client systems and writing your classroom papers. Keep articles in a loose-leaf binder for practicum materials.

Practicum Instructor: Suggest readings that will introduce your students to their practicum settings. Discuss at least one of the readings during supervision. Urge your students to keep up-to-date annotated reading lists and to share them with you and others.

Practicum Tutorial Teacher: Have students develop reading lists that are pertinent to their area of social work practice. Discuss the readings in your class that may have a broad application to social work practice, such as models, interventions, and outcomes. Ask each student to briefly present an annotation of an article and to provide a copy of the article for each student in the class.

✔ My personal reading list:

Author(s):
Year:
Title:
Type of Article:
Theme:
Key Findings:

Author(s):
Year:
Title:
Type of Article:
Theme:
Key Findings:

Author(s):
Year:
Title:
Type of Article:
Theme:
Key Findings:

Author(s):
Year:
Title:
Type of Article:
Theme:
Key Findings:

Author(s):
Year:
Title:
Type of Article:
Theme:
Key Findings:

Author(s):
Year:
Title:
Type of Article:
Theme:
Key Findings:

Author(s):
Year:
Title:
Type of Article:
Theme:
Key Findings:

Author(s):
Year:
Title:
Type of Article:
Theme:
Key Findings:

Chapter Two

*The most salient thought that comes to mind
is that learning in the classroom allows
for synthesis and reflection. Often in the
field, time pressures do not allow for this.*

— A Student

Learning the Pathways

You Can Only Get to Somewhere Else
by Starting Off from Where You Are...

B EFORE YOU CAN BE an effective professional social worker, you must have a beginning understanding of the learning process. Learning in your practicum is about four interrelated concepts: being, knowing, doing, and thinking:

Being: Developing appropriate qualities and attributes.
Knowing: Drawing upon relevant concepts, theories, and personal wisdom.
Doing: Using effective skills and behaviors.
Thinking: Applying the critical faculties of deciding, interpreting, judging, and reflecting.

Unlike other types of learning, social work education, especially in the practicum, begins with you. In developing all four aspects of being, knowing, doing and thinking, a competent professional evolves. To really accomplish learning within your practicum, you must be able to generalize from your particular setting so that you can *transfer your learning* from one social work setting, or context, to another. You need to be able to *use ideas to inform your practice* and to *generate theories* about what works from your practice experience. You also need to be able to step back from your work and *critically reflect on it*; and, perhaps most importantly, you need to *learn how you learn*. All of this will empower you to create and structure an environment conducive to your lifelong learning pathway. This requires far more than learning what to do in a particular practicum setting in order to get a job done.

What this really means is that you need to see yourself as a learner rather than seeing yourself as a worker, as a colleague, or as a new staff member in your practicum setting. It is important that your practicum instructor sees you as a learner as well. Seeing yourself as a learner involves some understanding of how adults learn and how various aspects in your learning environment and your practicum setting affect your learning. You can use all this information to help you plan to make the most out of your practicum experience.

LEARNING ABOUT LEARNING

Adults learn in many ways. Over the last twenty years teachers have come to believe certain ideas about adult learning and have applied them to social work educational programs and to their practicum settings as well. As the art and science of adult education has evolved, some of the assumptions about adult learning are being challenged by both adult learners and teachers. So what are some of these assumptions? You may have already questioned some of these myths in your own reflections about how you learn best.

Myths About Adult Learning

The are eight myths that sometimes surface when we start to think about how people learn. You must examine these myths for yourself when it comes time for you to start the learning process on your practicum journey. Let us now take each myth in turn, knowing full well they all interact with one another.

Myth Number 1

The first myth about learning is that many of us believe that it must be a joyful experience. However, meaningful learning often has elements of anxiety, frustration, and painful self-searching. Feelings of discomfort do not necessarily equate with a negative learning experience and, in fact, are often associated with powerful and memorable ones.

Myth Number 2

The belief that adults are self-directed learners is the second myth when it comes to understanding how people learn. However, many of us believe that adults can plan, conduct, and evaluate their own learning. The degree to which adults can or want to be self-directed depends on what is to be learned, how familiar they are with content, the subject, their skills, and the circumstances.

Myth Number 3

Some people believe that adults bring a lifetime of prior experiences that can be drawn on and used productively in the present learning situation. This is myth number three. In some cases the experience adults bring may mean they have entrenched ways of thinking, fixed ways of working, and bad habits and/or closed minds—which will all need to be addressed before new ways of being, knowing, doing, or thinking can be incorporated.

Myth Number 4

That adults know what they need to learn is the fourth myth. Often adults have a *general* idea of what they want to learn but they are not always sufficiently aware to know *specifically* what they do not know or need to know. In this regard many adults want and need the input of alternative views.

Myth Number 5

That there is one adult learning style is our fifth myth. Learning styles vary with the task and with the person. Adults frequently use various styles and approaches depending on what is to be learned, where it is to be learned, and when it is to be learned. Some adults have very strong preferences in their approach to learning, for others, which approach they select may depend entirely on the context.

Myth Number 6

The sixth myth is for us to believe that *satisfaction* is the measure of successful learning. The problem with using satisfaction as the gauge is that a satisfied learner could be someone who has learned little but is simply happy to get through the process without too many challenges or difficulties.

Myth Number 7

Myth number seven is that learning is a sequential and progressive building process. Learning sometimes proceeds this way, but it is also likely to occur in leaps and bounds with the occasional plateau. Some things cannot be learned by breaking them down into small steps and can only be learned by "swallowing them whole."

Myth Number 8

"Making mistakes means you cannot learn" completes the eight myths of learning. Mistakes have the potential for triggering significant learning, and sometimes we take great pains to cover them up. Learners need to be permitted to commit them, admit them, and submit them to scrutiny so they can be transformed into valuable learning events.

THE PATHWAYS TO LEARNING

Learning can occur in at least three ways:

✔ It can be intentional. You intend to learn to use a genogram in family work and you systematically used a genogram with the next five families that you saw.

✔ It can be incidental. While you were learning the technical elements of the genogram, you happened to learn that this tool creates opportunities for family members to talk to each other in different ways.

✔ It can be serendipitous. While using the genogram with a cross-cultural family, you discovered that "family of origin" traditions had far more influence on family rituals than you had ever realized.

For the most part, your learning will be intentional, but do not close your eyes to the rich opportunities to learn in your practicum setting that are incidental and serendipitous to the learning that you planned. Similarly, you can learn in a sequenced progression (step-by-step way) such as the use of a genogram in social work practice.

But there are other ways of learning as well:

✔ You can learn by trial and error. You tried doing the genogram by talking with only one person at a time. Next time you tried having both people provide similar information at the same time.

✔ You can learn in a spontaneous flash. All of a sudden you realized this pictorial representation provides you with a powerful way of understanding both the complexities in a family and interrelated themes.

✔ You can learn by accident. When using a genogram to understand a cross-cultural family, you learned that a genogram is a useful tool for assessing the intergenerational effect of alcohol in families.

✔ You can learn by mistakes. You waited until the fourth meeting to do the genogram and you learned that it is more useful to use it in the first meeting.

Although you will learn in many ways, you may need to pay attention to how you learn best and expand your pathways to learning.

Getting to Know Yourself

To expand your pathways to learning, you need to know about yourself. Who you are, how you learn, what you bring to your practicum setting, what you can contribute, and what you hope to accomplish all have relevance to your being an effective learner and, ultimately, an effective social worker. Developing self-awareness is part of the process of becoming a professional social worker and an effective practitioner. Understanding yourself, your learning style, and your personal, social, and cultural resources will help you begin.

Understanding your values goes hand in hand with understanding the values, ethics, and functions of the profession of social work. It is also an important preparation activity for practice. This self-knowledge can be helpful in understanding the ways your practicum setting may affect and influence your practice and how you may, in turn, impact your practicum setting. Your ability to learn also will be influenced by the values, beliefs, and traditions, the style of the organization, the types of clients served, and the current political, economic, or social conditions affecting your agency and practicum setting and the resources they have.

When your own values and those of your practicum setting interface, potential for conflict or tension can arise. This should lead you to question some of your deeply held beliefs. Failure to address the sources of tension can have damaging consequences on your learning and interfere with your progress. If there is a serious clash, you need to go to your practicum liaison or practicum tutorial teacher to discuss this further.

PRACTICUM SETTINGS DIFFER

Your practicum setting will usually take place in an agency of some kind or another. This is where your learning begins. Before your learning can begin however, you need to know that each practicum setting has its own style, its own clients, and its own resources.

Styles

Each practicum setting has a particular style. Some are more formal than others. Some people feel more comfortable and achieve more readily when guidelines are clear and discipline is imposed from within; others prefer a feet-on-the-table, sandwich-in-hand approach. If you are a feet-on-the-table person, are you also a leave-it-until-tomorrow person who needs structure to perform? Be honest with yourself from the beginning. If you settle happily into a relatively unstructured setting and do little because no one is making you do it, trouble is just around the corner. On the other hand, if you have a lot of self-discipline but just prefer to wear blue jeans, a less structured setting might suit you very well.

Large organizations tend to be more highly structured than smaller ones. The codes of dress and behaviors tend to be more rigid and well established. Correct procedures are defined and must be followed. Schedules, notices, forms, and memos abound. The two points to think about here are, first, whether you *like* structure and, second whether you *need* structure.

Clients

The type of client your practicum setting serves will obviously affect your learning. It is vitally important that you *inspect your prejudices and stereotypes.* You may think that social workers are not supposed to have prejudices or stereotype people but this is a myth and an illusion. We all carry certain attitudes toward people who are different from ourselves—attitudes that are usually brought forward from childhood.

Social workers are supposed to *acknowledge* their prejudices and recognize stereotyping to make sure that they do not adversely affect their work and relationships. For example, you may harbor a repulsion for persons who sexually abuse young children, or you may think that homosexuality is against nature, or you may believe that people who have attempted suicide have committed a sin. If these are your secret beliefs, it is far better to admit them to yourself, and pay attention to their impact on others. In order to become a culturally competent social worker, you will need to recognize this as an ongoing process involving continuous learning. If you would prefer to feel differently, you need to begin with self-assessment and self-insight.

Sometimes people want to become social workers in order to resolve their own difficulties or certain events in their lives. Be sure that you are not focused on a particular field or type of client problem to meet your own needs. If you have a personal agenda, it will cloud your clients' issues.

Resources

The term *resources* covers a wide spectrum, from practicum instructor qualifications to parking space for practicum students. In general, it refers to everything the setting provides that will help to build a good learning environment. Consider access, for example. The question, "Is it on the bus route?" may sound frivolous, but in fact "getting there" can be a major consideration for staff members, clients, and social work students.

Then, there is the matter of leaving, perhaps on a regular basis, to make home visits to clients. If home visits are encouraged, or even required as part of your practicum duties, you may need a car. Do you have a car or access to one? If you do, can you afford to use it given that your setting's mileage allowance may only cover paid employees? Who will pay for the doughnut you bought for Mr. Jackson, one of your clients, the first time you met him in the coffee shop?

What about overtime? A number of your home visits may have to be made in the evening. How many evenings are necessary on the average?

Is overtime rare, routine, expected, or required? Are you allowed to come in later in the morning if you worked the evening before? Will you ever be asked to work nights? Is shift work involved?

Next on the list is the question of physical resources. Will you have a telephone? If you have to interview clients, will these interviews take place in the six-foot area around your desk or is there a separate interviewing room? If there is a separate room, is it provided with equipment for taping? Audio equipment? Video equipment? Will you have time to try the equipment to get comfortable with it? Is there a one-way mirror so that you can observe other staff members at work and have them observe you? Is there a library? Libraries within practicum settings—often small, specialized, and close at hand—can be a valuable source of information. Is there a cafeteria? Can you smoke in it? If you cannot smoke in the cafeteria or anywhere else in the building, what do you say to Mr. Jackson who is a chain smoker, particularly during a crisis, and needs to "smoke up a storm" before he can talk?

All practicum settings, like all people, face problems from time to time. These problems are commonly related to funding or labor disputes and may not affect your practicum experience in any meaningful way. Occasionally, however, a crisis may mean that your practicum instructor has less time for you and temporarily has less interest in your learning than she does in the resolution of the crisis. Again, there are advantages and disadvantages to such a situation.

You get to watch the crisis unfold—a worthwhile experience in itself. You can catch a glimpse of the multitude of personal, professional, and political factors that affect your setting's functioning in the real world and are not taught to you in your classroom courses. On the other hand, your formal learning objectives may not be met to the same degree that they otherwise would have been.

You may be able to explore the potential of a possible practicum setting–based crisis during your first meeting with your practicum instructor. If the crisis is common knowledge—for example, if it involves a cut in funding or a looming strike which has been reported in the newspaper—you might make a sympathetic comment. If it has come to you through the grapevine, even more subtlety is required. For example, you might ask your practicum instructor what are the major issues or problems facing your practicum setting that you should know about.

Responses to such enquiries may vary from a defensive "we don't have any problems," to a humorous evasion, to a frank discussion of pertinent issues. Do not expect all of the problems to be displayed for your inspection. Your practicum instructor should, however, be prepared to discuss with you any problem that might relate to you as a practicum student. Frankness in this regard is a positive sign that issues arising later will be discussed openly. Much of this you will learn as you go along, but the more you can incorporate and understand in the beginning the quicker you will be able to get to the heart of learning in the real world of social work practice.

PLANNING YOUR LEARNING TRIP

Now that you have considered many of the factors influencing your learning, you need to examine how you can get started in your practicum setting. Whether you have been assigned your practicum setting, or you have selected it, sooner or later there will come a time when you will be sitting face-to-face with your practicum instructor. It may happen as a pre-placement interview before you start or it may be your first day in the setting. It is important that you think about this first meeting both from your point of view and from the point of view of your practicum instructor. Start with the questions that you might have on your mind and then consider questions that your practicum instructor might want to ask you. Finally, in planning to begin your practicum so that you get the best possible learning, you will need to think about yourself and what you bring to the setting.

Questions for Your Instructor

Below are a few questions that you might want to ask your practicum instructor during the first meeting.

- ✔ What are the kinds of things I will be doing and learning here?

- ✔ What systems will I be working with?

- ✔ Are you located in the same service area and in the same physical vicinity as I am?

- ✔ Will I have more than one practicum instructor?

- ✔ What is the largest single problem or issue facing your organization (e.g., agency or setting) that I should know about?

- ✔ What kinds of results would you like to see me produce as a practicum student?

- ✔ Where can I hang my coat, rest my feet, and have coffee?

Questions from Your Instructor

Below are some questions that your practicum instructor may ask you, that can help you prepare for your first meeting.

✔ What interests you most about this practicum setting?

✔ What do you believe you can contribute to this setting?

✔ Tell me about any social work–related volunteer or employment experience you may have had?

✔ What social work courses do you like best/least and why?

✔ How do you typically approach new experiences?

✔ What would you like to be doing five years from now?

SUMMARY

As you work your way through the guided exercises and activities at the end of this chapter, you are already beginning to realize that learning to be, to know, to do, and to think as a social worker is a journey. It begins with you. Enhancing your self-awareness and connecting who you are with what you know, what you can already do, how you think, and where you are going will ultimately put you on the road to understanding. After all, education is to learning as tour groups are to adventure. Your willingness to inquire into your background, values, personality, and other aspects of yourself will make you an effective learner. You can then combine this learning style with the conditions and context of your practicum setting, as this will also impact your learning. It is only after you admit what you do and do not know that you can focus on uncovering the information that acts as a road map to your understanding and learning.

Name: _____

EXERCISE 2.1: LAND MINES IN YOUR LEARNING FIELD

Type: Reflection — Application

Purpose: To consider the myths about how adults like you learn and how these myths may affect your assumptions about learning within your practicum setting.

Exercise: Read over the eight myths about adult learning. On the following page, write down specific examples from your own experience of learning.

Notes on Use

Student: After completing the following page, briefly note the themes emerging about your learning patterns or information gaps. Discuss in a group with your classmates.

Practicum Instructor and *Practicum Tutorial Teacher:* Have students discuss their beliefs about how learning comes about using their personal experiences. Identify where experiences converge and diverge; characterize themes that emerge for individuals and for the class as a whole. You may wish to provide examples from your own experiences with students.

✔ Learning is joyful.

✔ Adults are self-directed learners.

✔ Adults draw upon prior experiences and use them productively.

✔ Adults know what they need to know.

✔ Adults use one approach to learning.

✔ Satisfaction is the measure of successful learning.

✔ Learning is a sequential building process.

✔ Mistakes mean a failure to learn.

Name: _____

EXERCISE 2.2: MANY WAYS TO GET THERE

Type: Exploration — Application

Purpose: To explore the many ways of learning you have experienced.

Exercise: On the following page, provide an example of how you learned something by trial and error, incidentally, serendipitously, etc. Describe the effect that each experience had on you. Which of these would you describe as the most powerful learning experience? Discuss with others. Share in a group.

Notes on Use

Student: Write examples of each way you learned. Share with the class and discuss what you learned. Are some ways of learning more or less significant, valuable, or meaningful experiences for you?

Practicum Instructor and *Practicum Tutorial Teacher:* Have students identify examples of learning that occurred under the five situations named on the next page. Discuss the implications for their practicum assignments and experiences.

✔ Provide an example of past learning that was...

Intentional:

Incidental:

Serendipitous:

✔ Provide an example of learning by...

A sequenced progression:

Trial and error:

A spontaneous flash:

Accident:

Mistake:

Name: _____

EXERCISE 2.3: BEING AND KNOWING

Type: Exploration

Purpose: To identify personal qualities you possess that are likely to be resources for you as a social worker.

Exercise: List your personal qualities and examine whether or not your self-perception is congruent with the way others see you.

Notes on Use

Student: The completion of this exercise will help you become more aware of your personal qualities. Highlight those areas you think you want to develop, enhance, or change during your practicum setting. Mark qualities that will be a valuable resource for you in your practicum setting.

Practicum Instructor: Explore with the student at least two ways the student may develop, enhance, or change. Note those qualities that will be a resource for the student.

Practicum Tutorial Teacher: Ask students to share this exercise with at least one other student for feedback and discuss implications for learning in the practicum setting.

✔ List the qualities you have that could be an asset to you as a social worker. Describe ways or times these qualities are helpful to you and how, at times, they might be a problem for you.

✔ If you were to describe yourself to someone else, what would you say? If someone who knows you were to describe you, what would he or she say?

Name: _____

EXERCISE 2.4: CURVE AHEAD: STRESS CONTROL

Type: Reflection

Purpose: To examine your typical response to stressful situations.

Exercise: You need to consider how you have handled situations that have generated stress for you in the past and evaluate your reaction. Provide examples of stressful situations on the following pages and consider your response.

Notes on Use

Student: Starting your practicum experience is stressful and is just the first of many stressful situations you will encounter as a professional. What is stressful for one person may not be stressful for another. How you handle stress is crucial not only to your satisfaction in the profession, but also to your survival. Having a repertoire of coping mechanisms to draw upon in times of stress is a necessary survival skill.

Practicum Instructor: It is very helpful for students to discuss beforehand potential stressful situations they may arise in their practicum settings and ways to deal with this stress.

Practicum Tutorial Teacher: Discuss "burnout" in the social work profession and the need to deal with stress.

✔ Consider your typical response to a stressful or anxious situation. Be specific in your response. Assess what helped you cope in those stressful situations.

✔ How do you typically respond when others are in a crisis or in a stressful or anxious situation? Be specific in your response.

✔ Comment on and compare the similarity and differences when stress is personal or affecting others.

Name: _____

EXERCISE 2.5: DOING AND THINKING

Type: Reflection — Application

Purpose: To apply the knowledge gained from a learning style inventory to learning in your practicum setting.

Exercise: Complete one of the learning style inventories identified on the following page.

Notes on Use

Student: Understanding your learning style is an important aspect of self-awareness and will assist your learning about practicum opportunities and your impact on both your practicum instructor and your client systems. We all learn in different ways. Some of us learn by thinking about experiences, some learn more by actual hands-on experiencing. Others learn more from discussing issues. This exercise can help you maximize your learning style.

Practicum Instructor: Help your student select a learning style inventory. Identify and list ways students may have to adapt their learning style in the practicum. Discuss with the student and plan strategies for assignments. If you have not done a learning style inventory yourself, you may wish to complete the same inventory as your student. Discuss with the student similarities and differences in your learning styles.

Practicum Tutorial Teacher: Discuss the range of learning styles and learning style inventories with the students.. Discuss ways students can build on their strengths and, as learners, adapt learning style preferences in order to be more inclusive.

✔ Locate at least one learning style inventory and do it. Suggested inventories are: Gregorc, Kolb, and Myers-Briggs. Based on the learning style inventory and the self-awareness exercises, list your style or type as a learner. Identify how you can make them work for you in the practicum. List the ways in which you can go about learning what is required.

Gregorc, A.F. (1982, 1985). *Style Delineator: A Self-assessment for Adults.* Gregorc Associates, Inc., 15 Doubleday Road, Box 351, Columbia, CT 06237-0351, (203) 221-0093.

Kolb, D. (1984, rev. 1985). *Learning Styles Inventory.* McBer & Co., 137 Newbury Street, Boston, MA 02116.

Myers, I.B. (1985). *Myers-Briggs Type Indicator.* Consulting Psychologists Press, 577 College Avenue, Palo Alto, CA 94306.

✔ What can you tell your practicum instructor, your practicum tutorial teacher, and your practicum liaison about your learning style preferences?

Part Two

Mapping Out Your Itinerary

T HE TWO CHAPTERS IN PART TWO take you from your last-minute preparations into the very first few weeks of your beginning practicum experience. Planning is key to managing the uncertainties and unknowns involved in getting started. This is about orienting yourself and getting specific about mapping out the details of your practicum journey.

In a nutshell, the two chapters in this part are designed to help you chart an individualized path to follow as you embark upon your unique route to becoming a professional social work practitioner.

Chapter Three

Trip Tips

THE FIRST-DAY JITTERS

N O MATTER HOW CAREFULLY you plan for the first day of your practicum, some essential details will only occur to you the night before. For example, lunch. Will you accept half a sandwich and a carrot from your practicum instructor's brown bag if you do not take a lunch? Or, if you do take it, will you be able to hide it successfully when you discover that everyone else eats at The Food Fair next door? Should you go armed with a notebook and pen or should you assume that these will be provided? Will you look silly if you carry a briefcase or unprofessional if you do not?

Though these questions are trivial, they have a tendency to induce anxiety and cause you to arrive with lines of strain already imprinted on your face. The lines may deepen to grooves as your first day proceeds. The impression of carefree competence you meant to present will be gone, and worry over this may make the next day even worse. Coping with the beginning of the first day of your practicum experience involves using some basic survival techniques, finding out who are the people in your "neighborhood," and getting to know some things about your agency and the practicum setting in which you will be "learning how to do social work." This enables you to get oriented and to begin tracking your total learning process, which hopefully will stay with you for the rest of your professional life.

SURVIVAL TECHNIQUES

In the previous chapter, you began to identify some of the survival techniques that are part of your storehouse of personal management methods that you have acquired through your lifetime of experiencing new beginnings. You will be able to put these techniques to good use in the beginning phase of your practicum experience. Two of the many well-known techniques include using common sense in addition to keeping calm, cool, and composed.

Using Common Sense

Common sense is a much underrated virtue that is essential to social workers and sometimes ignored by social work students. For example, if your practicum setting has a cafeteria, or is two doors down from The Food Fair, you may not want to take a lunch. If it is miles from the nearest habitation, bringing a lunch is probably in order. In a similar way, the dilemma about briefcases can readily be resolved. First, do you have one? Second, do you have anything to put in it if you do have one? Third, is your agency and/or practicum setting a formal place where briefcases are valued, or is it a more relaxed place where plastic bags are *de rigueur*?

All this is not as silly as it sounds. The day-to-day problems you will encounter in your practicum setting are rarely of earth-shattering dimensions. They are usually *small* vexations that you do not quite know how to handle. Nowhere is the exact procedure written down, no one has told you what to do, and your practicum instructor is in a meeting. Even if she were not in a meeting, you would not want to bother her with anything so trivial but, at the same time, you are temporarily stuck.

If you make the wrong decision, do not worry. Applying common sense may prevent your own confidence from being eroded. It is therefore, important that you learn early not to agonize over trifles. Applying your common sense means making a decision that seems reasonable, and continuing with other tasks.

Using common sense is an underrated virtue. We urge you to use common sense in making judgments within your practicum setting. You can never have too much of it. Never let your heart guide your actions without allowing your brain to kick in your "common sense button." We want practicum students to become compassionate social workers who think before they act—tempered always with common sense.

Keeping Calm, Cool, and Composed

Being calm, cool, and composed is another useful technique. For example, you do not want to appear unprepared for your first day, but neither do you want to look as if you are moving from your dorm or apartment. Take a few things like this book and any useful material that your program's practicum director gave you. Leave the impressive textbook on research methodology and statistics; take your program's practicum manual and other practicum-related documents. Take the agency's and/or practicum setting's address, phone number, and the correct spelling and pronunciation of your practicum instructor's name. If you find that you have forgotten some vital piece of paper, there is always tomorrow or a fax machine or, if necessary, you could go home and get it.

Being calm, cool, and composed will help you survive the excitement and anxiety of beginning your first practicum experience. Do not lose sight of the fact that you are a beginning student in your first practicum setting. Keep repeating this to yourself.

You do not yet know where the washrooms are and it is all right not to know—for now, at any rate. There will continue to be, throughout your entire practicum experience(s), a host of other things that you do not know and cannot do. It is very easy to be overwhelmed by the sheer weight of your perceived anxieties—to feel that you are incompetent. Some students feel like they are imposters simply posing as eager, competent social work students and worried that at any time the real truth about them will be discovered. Feeling overwhelmed or like an imposter happens when you experience information overload, unfamiliarity with your surroundings and expectations, and being in the company of so many (even one) competent social workers.

A number of little errors can compound this feeling. You were introduced to four new people at a team meeting and got Joan confused with Doreen. You earned a raised eyebrow from your practicum instructor when you asked a question that was answered already in the meeting. If you make a mistake, you should think about it, but you need to see it as a learning moment, not as a failure.

But remember also that you are a student. You are allowed to make a mistake, to not know what to do, and to ask "already answered" questions. If you cannot admit this to yourself, and thus make allowances for yourself, you are failing to recognize the realities of your situation. Just say to yourself, "Be calm, cool, and composed," and you will soon be learning new skills, and as a result, will feel more comfortable.

We will now turn our attention to finding out who's who and what's what in your agency and practicum setting. Before doing this, however, it is important to remember at this point that your practicum experience is a learning one and you do not have to know everything the first day on-site. Finding out who's who and what's what involves three basic interrelated themes: getting to know your agency's rules and routines, getting to know some things about your practicum setting, and finding out about community resources.

GETTING TO KNOW YOUR AGENCY

During the first few weeks of your practicum experience, there probably will be times when nothing specific has been scheduled for you to do. Cherish such times—they may not occur again until you are drawing your Social Security checks—but also put them to productive use. For example, you can organize the information you have about your agency into a coherent system. The exercises that follow at the end of the chapter will help you understand the organization in which your agency and practicum setting are housed.

To understand the social services delivery system, your agency, your practicum setting, and how you fit in, you need to understand how your agency functions as a system. This is a complex task that requires a great deal of information and understanding of the dynamics of your agency. Read agency material, talk with your practicum instructor, and ask other professionals and staff in your practicum setting. Another helpful person to talk with is your practicum liaison.

History

It is useful for you to find out something about the history of your agency. How did your agency get started? Was it through a voluntary association of people determined to right some wrong? By statute? As an off-shoot of another organization? Or perhaps it was by metamorphosis—an evolution from prevention of cruelty to animals, for example, to prevention of cruelty to children. Often, the present characteristics of your agency can best be understood in the context of its history. It may have a large volunteer component because it began as a volunteer organization. When looking at your agency's current programs and policies, looking back to its history may help you to understand why certain things have or have not changed, or why the relationships between your agency and the community are the way they are.

Funding Base

It is also important to know about your agency's funding base(s). Depending on whether your agency is a public or private organization, money may be obtained from one or more of the following sources: federal government, state government, grants from various government departments, private individuals or foundations, fees paid by clients, donations, investments, and fund-raising events, to name just a few. Since it is usually true that whoever pays the piper calls the tune, an analysis of your agency's funding sources will enable you to see where control of its policies primarily lies. For example, you might find your agency described as a private, nonprofit organization administered by a voluntary board of directors. This means, in theory, that the people from the community who sit on the board are free to direct your agency's activities as they see fit. In practice, however, 90 percent of the funding may come from government grants or contracts and the board will obviously be anxious to accommodate the government.

There is nothing necessarily wrong with this, but it does mean that government policies, priorities, and regulations are very important even to private social service agencies. If you are to understand "the system" in which you work, and if you are to use it to benefit those you serve, you will need to know what regulations apply, what they really mean in terms of services to clients, and what the effects will be when they are changed.

Your understanding of the agency's funding sources (and those of the practicum setting as well) may lead you to a whole new investigation into government policies and legislation. It is important for you to find out about the relevant legislation that may affect social work practice within your agency and within your practicum setting and review it.

Policies

An agency develops policies to assist each social worker in carrying out social work practice within the agency. You can find out about the ways your agency wants you to practice by accessing its policy manual or policy handbook. Some agencies will have many different manuals because of the extensive laws and policies governing their responsibilities, such as a children's aid society and child protection work; or a hospital setting; or a women's shelter. These materials contain very important information about your agency's mission statement or reason for its existence, as well as the way it expects to fulfil its mandate through the programs and services it provides. Details are provided in the agency's policy manual about the ways social workers and others (such as students during practicum in the agency) must perform for accountability purposes. You should obtain a copy of the policies, and read the parts that pertain to your functions. Then discuss these practices with your practicum instructor to ensure that you fully understand what your mandate, role, and responsibilities are in order for you to be a good representative of the agency.

Organizational Structure

Another aspect of your practicum experience that you need to know about is the agency's organizational structure. Organizational structure refers to the linkages between and among departments and the lines of authority within departments depicted in the agency's organizational chart. Organizational structure is concerned with whether your agency is a large bureaucracy, whether it stands on its own, or whether it is a part of, or affiliated with, some other agency.

Look at your agency's organizational chart to discern the flow of information, communication, and the lines of authority. Who is at the head of the organizational chart? How many people are there in the organization? If there is a board, are they elected or appointed? Who has decision-making power? Do certain groups, departments, or programs have more influence than others? Have affirmative action policies or equal opportunity programs had an impact all the way up the organizational structure? The answers to these questions will tell you a good deal about how your agency functions.

Some of this information may not be readily available. You do not want to besiege your practicum instructor with questions about the expertise of the board of directors; your agency's manual may not tell you who influences whom. Nevertheless, if you make a beginning and you know what you are looking for, if you watch and listen and ask, this information will be revealed throughout your total practicum experience.

GETTING TO KNOW YOUR PRACTICUM SETTING

One of the most important things for beginning practicum students to know is the differences between an agency, a department, a program, and a practicum setting.

First, an agency is the umbrella under which various departments, and/or programs function. For example, a hospital is an agency with various departments to fulfil its overall mandate such as surgery, oncology, psychiatry, and social work. Your practicum setting could be social work which is one of the many departments of your agency.

Second, a department can have various programs. For example, a department of social work within a hospital can have various social work–related programs such as a discharge planning program, an AIDS awareness program, a pain management program, a biofeedback program for heart and stroke patients, and many other interdisciplinary programs such as child abuse teams, asthma clinics, and pediatric development clinics. Once again, your practicum setting could be one of the programs within a department (e.g., social work) within an agency (e.g., hospital).

In summary, know where you are on your agency's organizational chart and start to know what your roles and responsibilities will be during your practicum experience.

Finding Out Who's Who

Figuring out who's who means getting to know the staff, finding a few adequate support systems for yourself, getting to know your immediate environment, and getting to know the "no-no's."

Getting to Know the Staff

At first, you may feel anxious or uncomfortable with all of the unfamiliar staff who seem to know what they are doing. They know more than you; they are more experienced than you; they are professional social work staff while you are a social work student. Possibly they, too, are feeling some anxiety. You have bubbled eagerly into their lives, filled to the brim with new knowledge, new techniques, and new practice theories, when it may have been several years since they have seen the inside of a formal classroom.

In fact, new techniques and practice theories may be advantageous to them; one of the reasons students are welcomed is because they bring updated information from their social work programs to their practicum settings. Nevertheless, from a few staff members' points of view, anything that challenges the established way of doing things may easily contain a hint of threat.

Your next task is to introduce yourself as a social work student to staff members, tell them what social work program you are from, answer their questions as best you can, and then listen and observe. Try to link names to faces, with their positions and roles. Notice who sits with whom, who talks to whom, who avoids whom, whose opinion is respected, who says the least or most.

Observation of this kind will not only help you to know your colleagues more quickly; it will also help you to understand the personal and political nuances of your practicum setting ("the system") in which you must function. Such awareness is very important for you and all professional social workers alike. Your role on behalf of your clients often involves knowing who provides what services, where to go for information, and how to use "the system" for your clients' benefit.

You will also need to know how many staff are employed and the number (if any) of *volunteers* housed within your practicum setting. The counting of staff and volunteers is only a beginning. In addition, you may want to know what kind of qualifications and experience are required of staff members. What roles and responsibilities must they fulfill in various positions? What professional development training programs are provided for them? Do they stay for life or is there a high rate of turnover?

Similarly, you may want to find out what qualities are sought in the volunteers. How are they trained and supervised? What kind of work do they do? Are their services acknowledged through a volunteer day, a pin, an annual dinner, or merely a kind word? Does your agency or practicum setting revolve around the work of volunteers or are they peripheral or not utilized at all?

You will not learn all this during your first day. With any luck, you will be gradually introduced to people. This will give you time to write down your first impressions in your trusty journal (to be discussed shortly) so that Joan, once met, will be forever branded into your memory. If Joan happens to be a member of the support staff, remember that her work contributes to your ability to do your tasks. Members of the support staff can also be your best allies.

Finding Support Systems

If there are other students in your practicum setting, they will also be your support system—people in the same position as yourself with whom you can share your mutual anxieties, hopes, and uncertainties. At the beginning, it may *seem* that they know more than you or that they are more competent and better liked.

Perhaps this is even true. There will always be people who know more than you about something or other, whose personalities are brighter, whose intellects are more acute. Remember, though, that scientists who are not Einsteins still make contributions to science; writers who are not Shakespeares still make contributions to literature; and social workers who are not Helen Harris Perlmans still provide useful services to clients.

In all likelihood, the other social work students in your practicum setting are as overwhelmed and anxious as you are. If by some miracle they are not, you must remember that your practicum experience is not a competition. Your learning is based on your own goals, your agency's goals, your practicum setting's goals, your social work program's learning requirements, and your strengths and needs. It will not take place at the same rate, or in the same way, as someone else's learning, and it is not expected to.

You are not in a race with other social work students when all of you are running in different directions. Some practicum instructors will evaluate you on your overall improvement and give recognition to your personal circumstances; others will treat your performance in your practicum setting the same as it is treated in a classroom.

We will now turn our attention to finding out what's in your immediate environment. Before this can be done however, it is important for you to give some thought to the various staff members in your practicum setting and put faces to their names, roles, and responsibilities.

Getting to Know Your Immediate Environment

Before mapping out your itinerary, it is useful for you to observe your immediate surroundings. How welcome do you feel, how comfortable, how intimidated? If you feel comfortable, is your comfort due to your practicum setting's color scheme, the furniture, the artwork, the layout? If you feel intimidated, what is it about the place that makes it intimidating? What has been done to make the most of a tiny space, to compensate for a much-scuffed floor, to brighten a beige expanse of institutional walls? What turns a room into a good play therapy room, a safe room for anxious clients, a warm room for children, an encouraging room, a relaxing room? Are conversations audible through the walls? Will drapes reduce the morgue-like echo? What are the different effects of natural light, ceiling light, and shaded lamps?

Your exploration of your practicum setting should teach you a good deal more than the precise location of the coffee pot and washrooms. One important aspect of your surroundings is its openness and respect for the diversity of people coming through its doors. For example, are the pictures and magazines representative of the people who may be looking at them?

One of the ongoing tasks of your practicum experience—and, indeed, of your entire social work career—is to develop an awareness of your immediate environment. The next issue may be the location of your practicum setting within your agency. In a small agency, you might be located in the only office, with your practicum instructor. In large organizations such as hospitals, however, students commonly spend much of their time in departments other than the social work department—pediatrics or geriatrics, for example.

There are advantages and disadvantages to having your practicum instructor nearby. On the plus side, she will be there to sort out minor issues before they can turn into major ones and she may be in a position to give you frequent, hands-on feedback. On the minus side, you will probably be allowed less self-direction and you may not develop as much confidence in your own independent abilities.

Similarly, there are advantages and disadvantages to being located in a different department. In large organizations there are sometimes tensions between and among departments, and you may run the risk of becoming embroiled in territorial and personal disputes. In a hospital, for example, there may be a particular service to patients that social workers believe should be performed by social workers, psychologists believe should be performed by psychologists, and nurses believe should be performed by nurses. Such a situation is more than an organizational problem.

Whatever your opinion on the subject, if you feel yourself becoming involved in such disputes *talk with your practicum instructor*. If your instructor, herself embroiled, is unable to handle the matter, *talk with your practicum liaison*. Provided that you avoid embroilment, such episodes provide a wonderful opportunity to watch political maneuvering at work. Being placed in another department and working with people from different disciplines will give you a splendid chance to see how the disciplines mesh, and how people with different goals and loyalties manage to work together.

If you are placed in a different department than social work, be alert to the possibility that the lines of authority may be unclear or confused. Your work may be observed not only by your own practicum instructor but also by other members of the interdisciplinary team. Comments may float back. Approval of a physician may prove to be an important factor even though the physician's name does not appear anywhere in the official lines of "social work authority." Such a comparison between formal and informal hierarchical structures is a fascinating study that will serve you well in years to come. All in all, being placed in a different department has more potential benefits and more potential complexities than occupying the only desk in an agency's office.

Getting to Know the No-No's

Most of your practicum setting's rules, regulations, and routines will be explained to you during the first few days. If you have to take a public service oath or have a security check completed, you will be told about these procedures. The secrets of the many-buttoned telephone, the reluctant photocopying machine, the finger-chewing paper shredder, the communal computer printer, and accessing E-mail and the Internet will be revealed to you in turn, along with the ways of obtaining stationery, booking interviewing rooms, borrowing dictaphones, receiving messages, and so forth. Although initially confusing, all of this is basically quite straightforward; however, there are subtleties.

For example, you might discover that it is a no-no for social workers, especially students, to use the photocopying machine without asking permission from Marj. It may be another no-no to copy your term paper for your practice methods class. Havoc may occur when you use Ms. Tutty's coffee mug or remove Emmy's stapler. The remedy is to ask. Whenever you are in doubt as to the correct and accepted procedure, *ask*.

There will also be forms to be completed and reports to be written. For example, some practicum settings will not require you to turn in a time sheet, others may have you keep a detailed one. Your time sheet may not be a simple matter of arrival at 8:15 AM, departure at 4:30 PM, with half an hour for lunch. Instead, you may be asked what you did between 8:15 AM and 4:30 PM: How much of your time was spent in direct client contact, how much in working on your client's behalf, how much in administration, how much in educational supervision, and so forth. If you have not kept a daily record, much of your time sheet will be blank.

Soon you will have identified supports and have found out where the washrooms are. You will also, before too long, locate your desk, your practicum instructor's office, the photocopying machine, the stationery shelf, and the cold drink dispenser, along with other sundries such as the library, parking lot, and local pub (yes, we were students once too).

Some large social service organizations provide guided tours or maps to aid the wandering public. Whatever your route to discovery, pretend that you are not a social work student but a client seeking help. The intent of the exercises at the end of this chapter is to help you examine your first impressions of your new agency and practicum setting.

Now that you know all about your agency and practicum setting, we will turn our attention to the community in which they are housed. In short, the community houses your agency, which houses your practicum setting, which houses you. Oh, by the way, do not forget that your social work program is also involved in all of this "housing."

GETTING TO KNOW YOUR COMMUNITY

It is important, too, that you see your practicum setting (via your agency) as one link in a network of community services. You will need to know about other agencies because you will need to interact with them on behalf of your clients. If you write down the services each provides and integrate these services into an overall map, you will begin to see what problems within your local community are being addressed and where there are gaps.

If the services provided are to be useful, they should be based on the needs of the community. These needs, in turn, relate to the unique nature of the community in which your practicum setting is located—its ethnic or religious base, its poverty or wealth, its disparities in education and employment, its political views, and so on.

For example, clients obviously come from somewhere. Occasionally, they find your practicum setting themselves through the telephone book or through a friend, but often they are referred by someone else. The someone else may be a doctor, one of your clients, a schoolteacher, a relative, or a referral from another social service agency. In addition to knowing your agency and practicum setting, you need to know the community within which they operate. Most agencies provide service to people who live within a certain geographical area, and the geographical area served by your agency will provide you with some useful information. If your agency is funded by the county government, for example, it may serve people who live within the county limits free of charge and accept others on a fee-for-service basis as space permits. On the other hand, your agency may serve only part of a city, as some child protection agencies do, or be responsible for a large rural area or operate inside an entire state. This includes not only the other agencies and organizations that make up the network of social services in the area, but also the community at large.

Clients may also be referred to another agency after they have finished with you, or they may be receiving service from another agency at the same time they are coming to you. It is therefore important for you to know what is out there, not just in terms of social service agencies but in terms of the community as a whole.

For example, the community may seem to consist largely of small children. Probably this is an illusion, but it may be, in fact, a young community—or an elderly community, or a growing community, or a shrinking community. It may have a preponderance of mansions or apartments or cardboard boxes over heating vents. It may be conservative or revolutionary, violent or peaceful. It may have a strong religious or ethnic base.

In fact, most communities consist of diverse populations with multiple identities. You will need to discover the cross-cultural dimensions of the community and agency services. If you have little cross-cultural contact you may find it difficult at first to understand the pervasive role that race plays in the lives of people of color. Failure to acknowledge and address these dimensions of race and ethnicity can have damaging consequences for building trust and proceeding with your interventions. As a student exposed to issues of diversity you will be challenged to explore how your practices, knowledge, and skills might vary as a result of racial, ethnic, and cultural differences. Becoming racially sensitive and culturally competent is a learning process and a way of thinking and being.

All these factors and others will affect what services are most needed by the people within the community where your practicum setting is housed. The reason for collecting all this information is to give you an idea of what major problems exist in the local community where you will be placed. For example, there may be a large number of single-parent families who have problems related to housing and child care due to inadequate incomes. There may be youths with little education and no employment who are contributing to a rising crime rate. There may be a large percentage of the population with AIDS, and so forth.

The next step is to determine what is being done or can be done about these problems. Ideally, your practicum setting (via the agency) is part of the solution, and so are all the other agencies in the community's network of services. It is a good idea to list these agencies, making notes on what they do, whom they serve, and in what ways they interact with your agency and practicum setting. Think about the community characteristics, then compare the services that are needed with those services that are provided. This can prove to be very revealing and most useful in understanding your local community. The exercises at the end of this chapter will increase your understanding of how the agency and your practicum setting function within the community. This comparative information is valuable not only to you as a student but to your clients as well.

GETTING IT TOGETHER

In addition to getting to know the people within your agency, practicum setting, and local community, there are other activities that are involved in getting oriented to your first practicum experience. It is important to learn your practicum setting's routines for obtaining files, using the telephone and fax machine, advising the receptionist of your schedule, using government cars or keeping a record of mileage, keeping work/caseload statistics, documenting your work, taping and recording interviews, getting office supplies, and locating the coffee pot.

Another important orientation activity is introducing yourself to various staff members. Check with your practicum instructor about how social work students are to introduce themselves. Read some typical client files or case records to become familiar with service delivery, documentation, and standards in your practicum setting. Read the policy manuals.

Observe others: Sit with the receptionist; attend an intake interview; attend a case conference or a court presentation; observe a home visit with a social worker.

Again, finding the information you want will probably be a matter of picking up bits and pieces here and there. Manuals, pamphlets, and resource books will be useful. Your practicum instructor will be the primary source for this information, but you might ask other staff and your classmates—and, if it seems appropriate, your clients. Some clients know far more about community resources than some social workers do. Many of them have learned "the system" the hard way. They know what is out there and, most importantly, what is not.

If your practicum setting requires you to move to a new location, learn about the new town, hamlet, or community. Start a community file. What information sources are there? Find out about the local library and newspapers, obtain a copy of the local community services directory, list the health and social services information help lines, and so forth. See if a community needs assessment study has been done.

Begin to develop a list of resources or agencies that may be of use to you or your prospective clients. Sources for your list include the social workers, your practicum instructor, other practicum students, and your clients. All of these activities help in getting acquainted with the role of social workers in your practicum setting. In addition to familiarizing yourself with your agency, practicum setting, and community, you should make sure you know about safety policies and procedures.

AN OUNCE OF PREVENTION...

It is vital to raise the issue of safety early enough for you to take the necessary precautions to prevent any unfortunate occurrences. The first step is to find out about any agency policies regarding risk management and safety procedures. Some settings may have conducted detailed safety audits and have well-developed protocols, while other settings may simply expect you to use common sense. Examples include policies and procedures regarding building and office security, the management of violent clients, alcohol and drug use, home visits, transporting clients, and the reporting of incidents. Some settings provide safety training as part of the orientation to help students assess the potential for danger, de-escalate potentially threatening situations, develop self-defense skills, and minimize risk of exposure to illnesses.

Think about where you park your car or where you walk from public transportation in relation to where the office is or where your appointments are. If you are working after hours or in high-risk areas, think about the lighting, your visibility, alleys, doorways, and the access and exit routes. Think about how you carry your valuables, your money, identification, and credit cards and whether you should limit the cash and credit cards you usually have with you. Think about your appearance—do you look vulnerable or like a target? Are you taking unnecessary risks?

If home visits are expected, then what steps are taken to reduce the risk to your personal safety? Are you accompanied? If not, at least make sure there is someone who knows exactly where you are going and when you ought to be returning. You might want to invest in a cellular phone as a useful piece of safety equipment in case you get lost or have car trouble in an unfamiliar district.

When seeing clients, pay careful attention to their body language and potential for violence. If you have any reason for concern, notify someone else in the office, keep your office door ajar, and sit nearest the door. Do not ignore warning signs and pay attention to your "gut" feelings about the potential for danger. Familiarize yourself with communication skills for relating to angry or aggressive people and tune into the warning signs of violence.

It is important that you discuss safety issues with your practicum instructor and make sure you understand the types of risk to which you might be exposed. Consider the setting, consider the community, and consider your own susceptibility and "street smarts." This will heighten your awareness of the environment. Preparation will help you prevent, reduce, and manage the risks.

Harassment

Some safety policies include harassment, while in other settings harassment is a separate issue. However your school or practicum setting defines it, harassment is also an issue with which you need to be familiar. Sexual harassment is a type of harassment that deserves special consideration.

Sexual harassment is now recognized as a pervasive societal problem that manifests itself in virtually every setting: the workplace, community organizations, sports, and educational institutions. Sexual harassment is offensive, humiliating, harmful, and illegal.

There are many ways in which sexual harassment can be expressed, ranging from the very subtle to the most overt. It is important to note that it is the recipient of the behavior who decides if the behavior is unwelcome. What is a friendly pat on the shoulder to one person may be perceived as sexual harassment by another. In this regard, be aware that the laws focus on the impact of the behavior in question, not on the intent.

Any kind of sexual contact with clients by social work students is expressly forbidden. The same applies to social work students and practicum instructors. Unwanted sexual touching and suggestions from those persons who are in positions of power or authority are recognized as sexual harassment. Such situations will put you as a student in a difficult position. Fortunately, many universities, colleges, and social service agencies have policies to deal with sexual harassment, and as a student those policies are designed to protect you. Your setting may also have sexual harassment policies that can help you as well. It is vital for you to remember that there are steps for you to take and that you do not have to put up with any type of sexual harassment. Resolving a complaint of sexual harassment should, at a minimum, mean that the harassment stops and that there is no reprisal against you for having raised the issue.

The possibility of hitting some of these potholes or negotiating dangerous curves during your practicum may raise your anxiety and overwhelm you. One way to manage these feelings and all of this information is to track your journey.

TRACKING YOUR JOURNEY

During the first few days at your practicum setting, you will be given more information than you can possibly digest. The rules, titles, faces, and impressions will soon fade into a dusty haze. People whose names you have forgotten will expect recognition. Meetings will take place in rooms you cannot find. To some extent this is inevitable, but you can lessen the impact by writing things down. Start a journal. Even if you are not a "journal person" and have never kept a diary in your life, now is the time to begin.

Your journal can serve a number of purposes. At first, it may be a mixture of a list of questions to ask your practicum instructor, and a wailing wall. A little later, appointments will creep in: colleagues and clients you will have to see, telephone calls you will have to make, and therapy sessions you will have to observe. Make it a habit to document these things. If you make or receive a telephone call, note who you talked to, about what, when, and for how long. Also note what you promised to do as a result of the call, for whom, and by when.

Get a notebook that will serve as a daily journal or log for your practicum experience. The purpose of the journal is to keep track of questions, thoughts, feelings, ideas, as well as facts about you, your agency and practicum setting, your clients, and the processes occurring during your time in your practicum setting. Keep your journal up-to-date by regularly recording in it. It will become an invaluable source of data and learning as you proceed with your practicum experience. It may be very important when it comes time for your mid-term and final evaluations.

As the days go on, the entries you make in your journal will become more focused. For example, appointments, now more numerous, will be written in a separate appointment book. Anything to do with clients will be kept in the clients' files. You may need other files to separate out such things as therapy sessions observed with other workers, expense sheets, requisition forms, minutes of meetings, job-related legislation, community resources, and so forth. Your journal will now cease to be a general repository for every bit of information you can think of and will become a record of your learning process. All of your notes, articles, and so forth can then be placed in your loose leaf practicum binder.

The learning process will be discussed more fully later, but basically it will entail setting specific learning goals and objectives and accomplishing specific activities that will achieve those objectives. For example, one of your learning objectives might be to "develop group work skills in relation to rehabilitating cardiac patients." Your practicum instructor will want to know precisely what activities you have done to improve your group work skills (your objective), and it will help if you have devoted a couple of pages of your journal to this objective. For example, you might write down that on Monday you spent an hour with the group facilitator planning an agenda. On Tuesday, you reread a chapter from your group work textbook. On Wednesday evening, you spent two hours at a group meeting as an observer. On Thursday morning, you wrote up what happened during the group session and discussed it with the facilitator. By Friday, when you have your weekly educational supervision with your practicum instructor, you will have forgotten all about Monday unless you have written it down. If you have written it down, you will be well prepared.

SUMMARY

At the beginning of your practicum setting, you may find that there is both too much and too little to do. Small decisions you need to make may cause you unnecessary worry because you may be too anxious to make a good impression and to do the "right thing." If you use your common sense, compromise to some extent, and remember that as a social work student you are allowed to make a few mistakes, you will be able to put these worries into perspective.

At first, you may be overwhelmed with information and you might despair of ever being able to remember all the names, rules, and procedural details that everyone else takes for granted. The staff will help you if you ask them. If there other students in your practicum setting (or in another setting within the same agency), they will also help you.

There are two useful techniques for coping with information overload. The first is to keep a journal in which you can write your questions, take note of things you are told, and express your confusions. The second is to organize this information. Your journal will help you establish the habit of documentation and recording, which is very important for social workers. Organizing your information will help you to see your agency and practicum setting as "a system."

Understanding "the system" is an essential part of social work, because it is only through "the system" that you will be able to help your clients. If you collect information about your agency and practicum setting as you go through your practicum experience, the various parts and workings of "the system" will gradually fall into place. Basically, it is a matter of seeing the connections between such entities as funding sources, value systems, legislation, goals, services provided, and so forth.

Exploring your agency and practicum setting as a system in itself and as part of a larger community system will occupy many unscheduled hours at the beginning of your practicum experience. This includes making sure that you are aware of any potential risks to your safety and that you are familiar with the risk management and harassment policies and procedures of the organization. Attention to the cultural and racial contexts of the community and agency requires you to examine personal beliefs. The explanation of these assumptions will facilitate your growth and learning and your ability to be an effective social work student.

Nevertheless, after a while you might start to get impatient. It will be easier to contain your impatience if you remember that careful planning on the part of your practicum instructor is necessary to help you attain your learning goals. This planning takes time and, if you are prepared to wait, the results will be more satisfactory in the long run.

Soon you will need to write down your learning goals specifically in the form of a learning agreement. This will enable you, your practicum instructor, and your practicum liaison to see how well your goals are being met, in what areas you have progressed, and what remains to be covered. We will turn to learning goals in conjunction with learning agreements in the following chapter.

Name: _____

EXERCISE 3.1: FIRST IMPRESSIONS

Type: Exploration

Purpose: To tune in to your first impressions upon entering your agency and practicum setting.

Exercise: First impressions can be very powerful and affect us in many ways. Consider the physical appearances of your agency and practicum setting, the sights, sounds, and smells and their impact on you. Record your brief initial impressions in the space provided on the following page. Consider how your agency clients/consumers might experience entering those environments.

Notes on Use

Student: How did you experience the first day of your practicum? Discuss in detail and be honest with yourself.

Practicum Instructor: Ask about your students' first impressions of their practicum experiences. Use this to begin identifying your students' observational skills and point out how they can tune into the environment to gather information. Discuss with the students.

Practicum Tutorial Teacher: Give the students the opportunity to describe their first impressions of their practicum. Compare and contrast the impact of different practicum settings and first impressions of students and clients.

✔ My first impressions of the agency (note the visual impact, sounds, smells, and feel of the environment):

✔ My first impressions of the practicum setting (note the visual impact, sounds, smells, and feel of the environment):

Name: _____

EXERCISE 3.2: READ, READ, READ...

Type: Application

Purpose: To find out what kind of information is disseminated about the services of your agency and practicum setting.

Exercise: Obtain and read all of the material available about the services provided by your agency and practicum setting. Pamphlets, booklets, reports, and manuals are good sources of information. What information is disseminated to users of the agency's services? What information is disseminated to other resources?

Notes on Use

Student: Over the first few days that you are at your practicum setting, read everything you can about the agency in which your practicum setting is located. This will increase your knowledge of your agency and practicum setting and the community in which they function. These activities will help you get started and gain legitimacy. Assess these materials for their readability and utility. Record your responses on the following page.

Practicum Instructor: Ask your students to share their comments regarding agency and practicum setting materials. Share your own opinions. Discuss ways of improving the readability and utility of selected materials.

Practicum Tutorial Teacher: Have students describe their agencies and practicum settings. Exchange one piece of agency material and one piece of practice setting material for another student to comment upon and to have for his or her resource file.

Material Title: Intended for: Comments:

Name: _____

EXERCISE 3.3: VISITOR INFORMATION

Type: Exploration — Application

Purpose: To create a profile of the agency in order to have a sense of what it is all about.

Exercise: To develop the agency profile (this is not necessarily the practicum setting such as in the hospital), you may need to interview some staff members, read agency materials, and ask questions. This is an information-gathering exercise on your agency (not your practicum setting) as a system. Do not confuse your agency with your practicum setting. This is easy to do for beginning students.

Notes on Use

Student: Respond to each question on the following page and check with others for the accuracy of your answers. Write summary statements.

Practicum Instructor: Direct your students to the information necessary to complete the agency profile. Check for accuracy. Discuss your students' perceptions of their agencies now that they have gathered these profiles.

Practicum Tutorial Teacher: Collect the agency profiles from all students; copy and distribute to help other students know about various agencies and resources. You may want to include the previous exercise with this one in disseminating the information about the various agencies.

✔ Name of agency/organization:

✔ What is the mandate of the agency/organization?

✔ What is the goal of the agency?

✔ What services are provided by the agency?

✔ What is the value system that underlies the services in the agency?

✔ Describe a brief history of the agency:

✔ Describe the agency's funding base:

✔ Describe the agency's organizational structure:

✔ Describe the composition of staff (e.g., professional, administrative, technical, volunteer):

✔ Who are the users of the agency's services (categories of clients/consumers)?

Name: _____

EXERCISE 3.4: YOUR PRACTICUM SETTING

Type: Exploration — Application

Purpose: To understand the relationship between the agency and your practicum setting, develop a profile of your practicum setting as located within and related to the agency.

Exercise: This is an information-gathering exercise on your practicum setting and how it fits into the overall structure and mission of your agency. To complete this exercise, you will need to interview staff members within your agency and practicum setting, read materials and ask numerous questions.

Notes on Use

Student: It is extremely important to recognize that your practicum setting is located *within* your agency. Sometimes it can be a department within the agency. Sometimes it is a program within the department. If your agency provides only one social service (e.g., *only* foster care services), then your agency is your practicum setting since there are no other services offered within your agency. Respond to each category on the following page and check with others for its accuracy.

Practicum Instructor: Direct your students to the information needed to complete their practicum setting profiles. Check for accuracy. Discuss your students' perceptions of their practicum settings now that they have gathered these profiles.

Practicum Tutorial Teacher: Collect the practicum setting profiles from all students, then copy and distribute to help students know about various practicum settings within the various agencies. You may want to include the previous exercise with this one in disseminating the information about the various agencies and practicum settings that they contain.

✔ Name of your agency/organization (e.g., General Hospital):

✔ Name of your practicum setting within your agency (e.g., Department of Social Work):

✔ What is the mandate of your practicum setting (e.g., provide social services to hospital patients)?

✔ What services are provided to users in your practicum setting and how are these services complementary to the services offered by your agency (e.g., discharge planning—helps patients integrate into the community more effectively and efficiently)?

✔ What value systems underlie the services to users in your practicum setting (e.g., start where the client is, client self-determination)?

✔ Describe a brief history of your practicum setting (e.g., established in the hospital within the last 10 years):

✔ Describe your practicum setting's funding base (e.g., baseline funding out of the hospital's total operating budget):

✔ Describe your practicum setting's organizational structure:

✔ Describe the composition of staff (e.g., professional, administrative, technical, volunteer):

Name: _____

EXERCISE 3.5: YOUR COMMUNITY

Type: Exploration — Application

Purpose: To develop a visual representation and understanding of how the agency is clearly related to or linked with other systems in the community.

Exercise: By observing, analyzing, reading, and asking others, complete the questions on the following page.

Notes on Use

Student: To know your agency, you need to know and understand its relationship to the community in which it operates. This includes not only the other agencies and organizations that make up the network of social services in the area, but also the people in the community. You will need to carefully examine and integrate data at the interpersonal, environmental, and social-cultural systems level. Share your responses with your classmates and practicum instructor for accuracy.

Practicum Instructor: Have students complete the questions in order to develop an eco-map for the community in which the practicum setting and agency are located. Help students complete the community profile by placing the practicum and agency in the center. Discuss and consider the range of services and diversity of resources needed in relation to the population in the community.

Practicum Tutorial Teacher: Have students compare their community profiles and eco-maps. Discuss the emerging macro issues, such as service gaps, service duplication, ethnic or racial issues, housing problems, politics, and so forth by sharing the information.

✔ History and traditions of the community:

✔ Size, territory, and boundaries of the community:

✔ Major institutions and organizations in the community:

✔ Demographic characteristics of the community (e.g., age, gender, educational, ethnic, racial, religious groupings):

✔ Stability or transience of people living in the community:

✔ Economic, political, or social-cultural aspects:

✔ Other issues such as local politics, housing, and safety:

✔ Informal support systems (e.g., individuals, groups, or associations known for offering help, support, or material aid to others):

✔ Services needed:

Name: _____

EXERCISE 3.6: DIVERSE ROADS

Type: Reflection — Exploration

Purpose: To increase awareness and gain insight regarding diversity dilemmas.

Exercise: It is extremely important to explore possible sources or causes of oppression or discrimination. By talking to other social workers and your practicum instructor and reading agency policies, determine if the agency or organization is committed to culturally competent social work in practice as well as policies. Write your answers to the questions on the following page.

Notes on Use

Student: To provide you with specific knowledge and skills to be culturally competent, find the answers to the following questions. You may have to talk with different persons in the agency and community to learn the answers.

Practicum Instructor: To help students learn to practice cross-culturally they must have opportunities to understand how the agency practices with respect to diversity. Guide students to agency staff and policies to enhance their knowledge. Discuss with students. It is important that students feel there is a safe environment in which to explore diversity issues.

Practicum Tutorial Teacher: To enhance student opportunities to practice cross-culturally have them discuss as a group how their agencies indicate commitment to culturally competent social work practice. Clarify how these expectations translate into practice.

✔ Find out about the diversity represented in the client population served by the agency.

✔ Find out about the diversity represented in the professional and support staff of the agency.

✔ Find out about any agency equal opportunities or affirmative action policies.

✔ What steps has the agency taken to better serve diverse groups?

✔ How does the agency monitor its practice with respect to diversity?

✔ Has the agency identified any barriers to access or taken steps to remove or reduce them?

✔ How will you gain exposure to, and have opportunities to work with, a variety of people across a range of differences?

Name: _____

EXERCISE 3.7: YOUR PRACTICUM MAP

Type: Application

Purpose: To have a visual representation of your agency, your practicum setting, your local community, and the environment in which they all operate.

Exercise: You will find that each way you organize information creates new information and new understanding. It is easier to perceive a whole picture with a map. An eco-map provides you with the means to see patterns and understand connections. Draw an eco-map of your agency, your practicum setting, your local community, and the environment within which they operate.

Notes on Use

Student: Draw an eco-map depicting your agency and its relationships and exchanges with other systems in the larger community in which it is located. Use the previous three exercises to depict your agency, your practicum setting, your local community, and the environment in which they operate. Use a solid line for an ongoing relationship. Use a dotted line for strained relationships. Use no line where there are no relationships. Indicate relationships that are positive, stressful or tenuous, sources of energy, and others that you think are important.

Practicum Instructor and *Practicum Tutorial Teacher:* You may want your students to do this near the beginning of their practicums and again toward the end. Compare the two versions of the eco-map as a way of discussing all that has been learned.

✔ Draw an eco map of your practicum setting (in the center), agency, and other community systems. Include your legend for the connections between various systems and people. My practicum eco-map:

✔ My practicum eco-map continued:

Chapter Four

The Power of Planning

CREATING A LEARNING ENVIRONMENT TAKES COMMITMENT

CREATING A UNIQUE LEARNING ENVIRONMENT for yourself is very much like planning your itinerary for a trip you will take soon. The agency where your practicum setting is located is the city you will visit and the local community is the countryside you travel through as you drive to your destination—becoming a competent social worker. Planning for the trip is essential. Where to eat? Where to stop? How much luggage? Do I need 24-hour roadside emergency assistance? All these questions require planning so that schedules are anticipated and unscheduled stops are minimized. While roadside attractions are to be admired, you must reach your destination in a very short period of time.

In your roles as explorer, adventurer, passenger, tourist, and visitor, you are free to travel the many different routes to your destination, at times by yourself or with someone else. You may find yourself speeding along the highway. At times you may wander along the old coastal road to see different scenery. Of course you will plan to stop along the way, maybe at an intriguing roadside cafe, or a waterfall, or a quiet roadside park. The more planned stops you make the more you see. Unplanned stops can be annoying, frustrating, and downright time consuming and even interfere with the expected time you need to reach your final destination.

Whichever road you choose to travel, you will experience to varying degrees the terrain, the sights, and the delights of your journey. Of course you will try the food and talk to the local residents about your trip. You may even plan to stay over in various places, to participate first hand in what it would be like live in the countryside. Plan to visit those places that are especially well known in the locale. Talk to people who work and live in the different places. Find time to sit down, rest, and observe the environment.

In this way you will appreciate the unique qualities of your trip, whether it is the scenery or the visits to specialty shops, galleries, or monuments. It will be unique, and you will need to stay in contact with the tourism office, and the tour organizer and tour guides—your practicum director, practicum instructor, and practicum liaison—to make sure your trip is well planned.

Initially you will become familiar with the map you have drawn for yourself, but you will definitely need help in map reading. The tour organizer, your program's practicum director, will locate experienced personal tour guides, your practicum instructor and your practicum liaison, to make your trip a memorable and learning one, so that you do not get lost navigating. The three of them will help map out a course based on your needs and experiences.

Of course, you will have some responsibilities for planning many parts of your itinerary. Defining learning goals and objectives, suggesting specific assignments or opportunities that will help you get to your final destination, are also a part of your responsibilities. You are in part responsible for organizing your learning assignments to accommodate the schedules of all those involved. And you are in part responsible for coordinating these assignments so that they form a coherent pattern of your overall learning needs.

The designated itinerary is ready. It tells you—the traveler—what is to happen, why it is to happen, and how the parts of your trip are connected. The most important part, the anticipated enjoyment of your trip, is yet to come.

Your individualized learning agreement in addition to your program's practicum evaluation form (see Appendix B) is the map for what you will learn via your learning agreement. Sometimes learning agreements are called *educational plans* or *learning contracts*. Learning agreements provide the rationale—the "why" parts—and are the goals you want to achieve while you are in your practicum journey.

Reaching those goals is why you are here, why your journey has been set in motion, and why your tour organizer (practicum director) and your two tour guides (practicum instructor and practicum liaison) are prepared to map out a route to make your trip a success.

MAPMAKING INFLUENCES

Mapping a learning environment is extremely important to your overall learning experience while you are on your trip. Your learning environment is co-created: It involves *you* in developing learning goals that are related to your social work program's objectives and in partnership with what your agency and practicum setting can provide you in the way of actual experiences, guided by Social Work's *Code of Ethics* (Appendix A). But other mapmakers—such as other practicum instructors, your classmates, other client systems, and other professionals—are also involved in co-creating your learning environment. Obviously, the ideal environment is one where you learn best. There are other influences that must be considered and they are discussed below.

Social Work's Code of Ethics

The National Association of Social Workers has a *Code of Ethics* (see Appendix A), as does the Canadian Association of Social Workers, the British Association of Social Workers, and the Australian Association of Social Workers, which delineates principles of professional conduct. The applicable *Code* should be read, reread, and followed. The *Code* is there to guide ethical behavior but it cannot make decisions for you; you will learn to make your own professional judgments. During your first practicum experience, you will likely be required to demonstrate (Appendix A):

> ... values consistent with those of the profession and an understanding of and commitment to ethical standards.

The above refers to your ability to use values to guide your practice. Most probably, you will be quite able to discern value conflicts and ethical issues and use your professional judgment and the *Code of Ethics* to make good decisions. If you do make a mistake such as releasing a client report without authorization, *discuss it with your practicum instructor.*

The "Confidentiality and Privacy Section" of the *Code* states (Appendix A):

The social worker should inform clients fully about the limits of confidentiality in a given situation, the purposes for which information is obtained, and how it may be used.

You may believe that Ms. Banks will not tell you that her husband is abusing her daughter if she knows you will report the abuse to child protection services. Therefore, in an effort to protect her daughter, you may be tempted to get the information out of Ms. Banks without mentioning "child protection services." Such devious manipulation of Ms. Banks is unethical even though it is done with the best of intentions. As the old saying goes, "the road to hell is often paved with good intentions." Always be careful of "your good intentions." You must consistently blend your good intentions with good responsible practice. Never let your heart cloud the judgment of your brain. Think, then act.

When conflicts like these arise, consult your practicum instructor and/or your practicum liaison at once. It is very easy to be drawn into a situation where you cannot be honest with your client, you are afraid to tell your practicum instructor exactly what you did, and you are not very happy with yourself. The *Code of Ethics* provides you with one type of map to guide your learning during your practicum experience. Your social work program, via the practicum director, your practicum instructor, and practicum liaison, provides you with another.

Your Program's Objectives

Each social work program will have more or less similar objectives with regard to the training and education of its students. Nevertheless it is important for you to be clear what your specific program is emphasizing—such as generalist practice objectives; micro, mezzo, or macro practice objectives; community practice objectives; research; or even some familiarity with each of the objectives. Different competencies are required for different objectives, and you will need to acquire knowledge in the area your program thinks is best.

Some of this information will be in your student handbook, in your practicum education manual, or available from your practicum course outline. All social work programs have a common set of values and attitudes that students are expected to hold and demonstrate through various course content and practicum experience.

YOUR USER-PARTICIPATION MAP

You define your learning goals when you write your learning agreement. To some extent these goals will be defined for you, because your social work program will have certain minimum standards, stated in learning objectives and outcome criteria, that you are expected to achieve in your practicum setting. Your learning goals should always be linked to the criteria that you will be evaluated on. You can add as many learning goals as you, your practicum instructor, and your practicum liaison, believe would be suitable for you.

For example, by the end of your first practicum setting, you may be expected to know how to *"effectively function within a professional context"* (see Appendix B). Since this goal can cover a multitude of competencies, specific objectives may be delineated to describe more precisely the ways in which you are supposed to *"effectively function within a professional context."*

At a very basic level, it means that you present in a professional manner and do not interrupt others at staff meetings. At a somewhat higher level, it means that you do not show disapproval of a client who has institutionalized her mother because you believe that adult children should care for their elderly parents.

Your practicum instructor will be asked to assess you on this particular ability, and her assessment will probably depend on a number of your specific behaviors. The suitability of your manner will be taken into account, as will your ability to argue a point without implying that people who oppose you are wrong, your ability to work with others from *their* value base, not *yours*, and so forth.

You will eventually have to look at yourself and see how you think you rate in this particular area. If you think you are doing okay, and your practicum instructor and practicum liaison agree with you, this is good news. If you think you may have a problem, try to define "the problem" more precisely. For example, you may find that you can never present an opinion to a group without alienating at least half of the people present. If this is the case, it is probably your presentation, not your opinion, that is at fault; therefore your learning objectives may be to remedy the matter. To repeat, defining your learning objectives is part of writing a learning agreement.

Defining Your Learning Objectives

Phrase your learning objectives in educational terms. Your writing ability definitely counts as a behavior, and the impact of your words on others is one of the things you are expected to recognize. For example, you might write a learning objective as, "*learn to participate in group discussions in a positive manner.*" Having written this objective, you have to take some action to prove to your practicum instructor that some learning is taking place. Pick an issue that is close to your heart, preferably controversial, and plan how you could present your case in a respectful, professional, and reasoned manner.

Ask your practicum instructor to role-play with you so that you can learn to respond to opposition in the confines of her office. If you do not feel comfortable in your practicum instructor's office, ask someone else instead (and make a mental note that the relationship between you and your practicum instructor needs to be further explored).

You will derive some of your learning objectives by carefully going through your program's practicum evaluation form (see Appendix B) to see exactly what it is that your social work program expects of you. Other objectives will occur to you when you think about what your practicum setting does and who it serves. For example, suppose you are required to demonstrate "*the ability to take initiative toward increasing knowledge and skills relevant to performance demands.*" This means that you do not blindly complete assignments and wait after each task to be told what to do next. Instead, you play an active role in your learning by suggesting to your practicum instructor that this or that activity on your part might help with such and such objective. You can use information from your learning styles inventory to identify the kinds and types of practice assignments with which you need experience.

You may find that you are quite incapable of suggesting anything to your practicum instructor: You are not able to assert yourself. Your learning objective, therefore, will be "*to become more assertive.*"

After you have written this down, there is more to be said. How will you know when you have become more assertive? What behaviors on your part will tell both you and your practicum instructor that this specific objective has been achieved? Some behaviors will be evident since it was your lack of assertiveness that prompted the learning objective in the first place. Your objective now is "*to make appropriate suggestions to your practicum instructor regarding your learning activities.*" Your other objective is "*to participate in group discussions in a positive manner.*" Yet another objective is "*to maintain focus on clients' problems or maintain focus on issues of concern with the mothers against drugs group*"—that is, not to allow Ms. Banks to lead you off the topic.

Your practicum instructor will be able to assess these more precisely stated objectives. She can count your appropriate suggestions; she can tell from your process recordings (to be discussed) when you are zeroing in on Ms. Bank's most important issues. You have managed to work toward an overall learning objective—becoming more assertive—in a number of concrete activities.

For example, one of your learning goals may be *"to acquire interviewing skills"* and one of your specific learning objectives related to this goal may be *"to learn to define the client's problem in a generalist family service setting."* With this objective in mind, you can coordinate a number of activities: reading whatever you can find about defining client problems; observing other social workers define problems with their clients; watching relevant videos; recording and discussing with your practicum instructor your attempts to define problems with your own clients; having your practicum instructor role-play a client who is absolutely determined not to tell you why she came to your practicum setting (or agency); and exploring in theory the many barriers people have to solving problems.

Remember, words may have different meanings, so you will want to be sure you and your practicum instructor draw the same meaning from the words you use in your learning agreement. Keep in mind that good description will be a map to good instruction.

Organizing Your Learning Agreement

As you can see from Figures 4.1 through 4.4 on pages 106 to 109, there are many ways of organizing your learning agreement. The organization may follow your program's practicum evaluation form or may be prescribed on a form all its own. On the other hand, it may be left up to you, your practicum instructor, and your practicum liaison to determine its shape. Our four simple examples of learning agreements have been deliberately taken from different practicum settings to reinforce the point that your learning agreement is an *individual* one. The practicum evaluation form is different for each social work program, and the learning agreements will be different for each student. You are likely free to organize your learning agreement in any way that appears reasonable, unless your program has a specific format it requires you to follow.

Probably the most sensible way to start organizing your individual learning agreement is to follow the headings and subheadings on your program's practicum evaluation form (if it has one, that is). You will have a number of learning objectives under one goal, and you may find that some of them have to do with using theoretical knowledge and some of them have to do with acquiring practice skills. For example, you may be required to function effectively utilizing knowledge-directed practice. This requires that you will have *"demonstrated the ability to engage others and identify problems or concerns,"* and more specifically that you *"learn to identify each persons' problems or issues of concern."*

Achieving this learning objective is a very practical matter. You have to interview Ms. Banks, form a relationship with her, and persuade her to divulge the real reason she came to your practicum setting (or agency). You may be required to have *"demonstrated the ability to articulate a comprehensive assessment."* Part of this is practical—you have to complete an assessment on Ms. Banks—but part is theoretical. You have to know, from theory, what information about Ms. Banks and her family should be included in an assessment. Your learning objective here might be *"to learn how to formulate a comprehensive assessment,"* or, *"to complete an integrative assessment using at least two different data gathering methods."*

Under one heading, or goal, you can easily end up with a number of practice-oriented learning objectives and a number of objectives that are more concerned with theory. It may seem worthwhile then to group them under the subheadings: *Theoretical and Practical*, or *Conceptual and Technical, Skill Development*, or *Personal*, or whatever words appeal to you. Do not forget that your individual learning objectives should be related to the nature of your practicum setting as well as to the standards set by your social work program. For example, the information contained in a comprehensive assessment of Ms. Banks will depend on why you are assessing her situation. If you are working in a nursing home and Ms. Banks is applying to become a resident, you may need information about her financial status, her medical history, her likes and dislikes, information on local community programs, and so forth.

If Ms. Banks is to enter a drug rehabilitation program or a therapy group for sexual abuse survivors or a foster parent training program, the required information will be different. You may want to write your learning objective about assessments more specifically in order to reflect this. For example, your objective might be *"to learn how to evaluate a foster parent support group."*

Some of your learning objectives will not be concerned with either practical or theoretical learning. Instead, they will refer to personal development, and you may wish to put them under a separate heading. For example, you might list your objectives about becoming more assertive under the *Personal* heading. Keep in mind, however, that your personal objectives need to be related to your professional development as a social worker. Your learning agreement should also include the following administrative information: the number of days per week and the number of hours per day you will spend at your practicum setting, the frequency and length of supervisory conferences, supervision method (e.g., individual supervision, peer supervision, or group supervision), the number and type of case or project assignments you are to be involved with over a specific period of time, documentation and recording procedures expected by your practicum setting, and any special arrangements you have made. The most important thing for you to remember is that your learning agreement is an individual one and should thus be written with this in mind. The exact format will vary from program to program, student to student, and practicum instructor to practicum instructor.

All this could be organized under another heading, *Strategies* or *Activities*, for example. After all, the strategies or activities you use to help you achieve your objectives include such things as planned supervisory conferences, videotaping your interviews, process recordings, and so forth.

Examples of Learning Agreements

Figures 4.1 through 4.4 present four distinctively different examples of learning agreements for students in institutional (Figure 4.1), psychiatric (Figure 4.2), shelter (Figure 4.3), and community settings (Figure 4.4). These are only examples; your learning agreement is a personal map developed by you, with help from your practicum instructor and your practicum liaison, along with other guidelines such as the relevant *Code of Ethics*, your program's objectives, and the opportunities that are made available to you within your practicum setting. Nevertheless, these four simple examples may serve as a guide when it comes time for you to write your own learning agreement.

Refining Your Learning Agreement

When you have defined and organized your learning goals and objectives, you will have to submit them for final approval by your practicum instructor and your practicum liaison. Of course, it is more practical to discuss your learning agreement with these two people as you go along; use their feedback to revise and make additions. Occasions will arise, however, when your practicum instructor and your practicum liaison believe your objectives are unrealistic and you, of course, believe that your practicum instructor's and practicum liaison's expectations are too low.

Remember that if your learning experience does not proceed precisely as expected, or if new opportunities and needs arise, objectives can be revised at any time during your practicum.

We suggest, therefore, that you accept the advice of your instructor and liaison at the beginning. If it turns out that you have set your sights too low, and/or in a direction that is slightly wrong, you can rectify this situation later.

LEARNING AGREEMENT

Conceptual (Theory Development)

• To learn what being a resident means (e.g., possible loss of dignity, feelings of being controlled, fear of unknown) • To examine institutional values versus individual personal values and if or how they are reconciled • To understand defense mechanisms that arise when people feel threatened • To gain an understanding of the theory behind group dynamics and individual counseling • To understand the social concept of "deviance" and to examine it in relation to substance abuse and prevention programs • To become aware of the roles of the various voluntary agencies (e.g., AA, Salvation Army) and how they relate to the institution and substance abusers • To understand the role and purpose of the bureaucracy and hierarchy of the institution and look at what effect this can have on staff relations, service delivery, and clients

Technical (Skill Development)

• To develop skills in working with a patient group (where focus may be both educational as well as therapeutic) • To acquire skills for individual counseling • To develop assessment and diagnostic skills (in particular, assessment when intensive intervention is indicated) • To develop skills in staff groups such as (1) presenting group dynamics and process and individual case studies, (2) chairing a meeting, (3) giving feedback to other staff, and (4) presenting relevant information to staff • To examine personal and professional roles—can they be combined or must they be separate? • To participate in therapeutic discussions with colleagues, offering a social work perspective and gaining from their expertise • To become skillful in the role of a group worker

Community and Project Work

• To become involved in relevant projects and community work where time allows

Strategy

• Educational supervision for receiving feedback • Tape recordings of client interviews • Summary recordings on charts • Report writing (identifying specific reports) • Tape recordings of supervisory sessions

FIGURE 4.1   Example of a Student Learning Agreement for an Institutional Setting

LEARNING AGREEMENT

Aim

• To work as a member of a professional team in the role of a social worker in a psychiatric setting • To gain an understanding of what it means to be a social worker in this agency • To understand why a social worker acts/reacts/interacts to situations as they arise • To develop a basic theoretical framework to which further thoughts and actions can be related • To establish how this agency fits into the community, and then, from the agency's viewpoint, where the profession of social work fits in

Conceptual (Gain an Awareness of the Teamwork Model)

• To look at models of community interaction and how they apply to this agency • To gain knowledge of community functioning, that is, how the agency works for various sectors of the community, appreciation of associated agencies, knowledge of resources available • To look at how different people cope or do not cope with their situations; to establish models of coping, develop a style of assistance that suits myself • To become proficient in understanding of psychotropic medication and DSM-IV diagnoses

Operational (Develop Skills)

• Relating to people • Constructive interviewing (i.e., relating as a helping person to a client on a professional level) • Relating as a professional to other professionals in the team (look at networks) • Working as a member of an interdisciplinary team for the sake of the client • Report writing, fulfilling the accreditation standards of the agency • Developing assessment and diagnostic skills

Personal

• Aiming to feel confident in dealing with people in general • Being able to deal with various people with differing problems and different degrees of problems, with confidence • Facilitating personal growth, self-development • Gaining an understanding as to why one thinks a certain way—becoming aware of own actions and the effect that background and upbringing have on these actions

Strategy

• Weekly supervision sessions • Weekly review of cases to see if they are being dealt with in the most beneficial way for the client • Diary for planning weekly activities, as well as a record of tasks completed • Agency visits • Taping interviews

FIGURE 4.2   Example of a Student Learning Agreement for a Psychiatric Setting

---

LEARNING AGREEMENT

S = Student

PI = Practicum Instructor

Aims

• S aims to increase knowledge of available and relevant community resources and to develop skills to understand appropriate use of the referral process to these resources • S aims to gain an appreciation and understanding of the roles played by other professionals (e.g., police; housing authority; welfare; counselors; court) in the delivery of services within the shelter • S aims to enhance understanding of the policies and practices of the social work staff by undertaking relevant reading and by discussions with all staff • S aims to enhance skills in identifying client problems and in building and utilizing repertoire of interventive techniques • S will aim to increase the knowledge of helping processes through reading and discussions with staff • S will learn feminist model of practice

Strategy

• S will arrange to record two or three interviews with clients and/or their families. These clients and families will be informed of the reasons for the recordings, asked if they will participate, asked if they wish later to listen to the recordings and/or to be present when they are erased. S and PI will subsequently analyze content and process of such interviews for the purpose of increasing S's professional social work knowledge and skills • S will ask PI to be present during two or three interviews, either in the shelter or during a home visit. Both S and PI will subsequently analyze the interview with respect to its content and process, thereby increasing S's professional knowledge and skills • S and PI will regularly undertake process recording; that is, S will record the interviews and inform PI of the content, and together they will examine the processes operating during the interviews • S and PI will spend one hour per week in educational supervision, S taking responsibility for selecting topics for discussion for each session • S and PI will review this agreement every three weeks

---

FIGURE 4.3   Example of a Student Learning Agreement for a Shelter Setting

LEARNING AGREEMENT

Conceptual

• To test the center's ideas in the development of an individual perspective and conceptual framework for community work practice • To examine various models of community development work and assess their applicability to the center • To understand the unique structure of this community and relate this understanding to various concepts of community work and changes occurring in communities • To understand the basis of community involvement in the center's management and the relationship of the worker to the management committee

Operational

• To develop communication skills in working with community members, as participants at the center, as members of management committee, and as leaders in the community; in working with other staff at the center and workers in other agencies; in report writing and submission preparation; in contacts with the media and the public presentation of the center; and in negotiating with external agencies • To develop skills in recording and evaluating one's activities and the work of others in the community setting • To identify formal and informal networks and utilize them for the benefit of the center • To develop an initial familiarity with the basic processes of some of the different approaches to community work

Personal

• To identify and explore own beliefs and views about community work as a strategy for change • To arrive at a perspective on own role as a community worker in the center, in the surrounding community, and in society at large • To learn to work with people and tasks in potentially uncomfortable situations • To experiment with different behaviors in different situations, leading to the development of a personal style as a community worker and to become comfortable with that style

Strategy

• To read as widely as time will permit; prepare at least three book reviews for discussion with my supervisor • To maintain a daily diary and prepare process recordings on activities undertaken • To plan a program of discussions with center workers and selected members of the community • To prepare a proposal of planned work, together with a justification of the activities planned, for each supervisory conference; do an analytical review of the previous week's work

FIGURE 4.4   Example of a Student Learning Agreement for a Community Center Setting

THE MAPMAKERS

Once you have developed your practicum map—that is, decided on your learning goals and objectives—your next consideration will be the roles of the various mapmakers.

Your Practicum Instructor

A key factor in establishing a relationship with your practicum instructor involves understanding and negotiating differences in expectations and attitudes due to different ethnic, cultural, or religious backgrounds. Another factor is concerned with age and gender differences; another is concerned with stresses due to handicap conditions. Still other issues of significance are how each party learns, how personalities mesh or clash, and how each one deals with authority. A further factor is the matter of organizing and managing supervisory conferences. All these will be discussed when we talk about how you can manage your practicum experience, starting with the next chapter.

An important aspect in establishing a relationship is your understanding of your practicum instructor's responsibilities. What is her role in the agency and practicum setting apart from being your practicum instructor? Does she get any sort of work load reduction during the time she is your practicum instructor or is she expected to fit you into to her existing work load? There may be times when she is not available to help you but if you know what else is on her plate you can make allowances for these times.

A good relationship depends to some degree on knowledge. If you learn about the particular issues your practicum instructor may be facing at your practicum setting, you will not only add to your own experience but you will be able to be appropriately understanding when the occasion arises.

Occasions may also arise for an exchange of more personal information about families, hobbies, mutual acquaintances, past experiences, and so forth. A student and a practicum instructor who both belong to a specific social action group can easily form a deep and satisfying bond, for example. Try to find common ground with her.

Your Practicum Liaison

You may see your practicum liaison occasionally or on a regular basis, depending on whether or not your practicum tutorial is taught by her. She is the person to talk to if you have an issue you cannot resolve with your practicum instructor. Even if you do not have a problem, it is a good idea to keep your liaison informed of your progress, because she will likely be involved (to various degrees) in your mid-term and final evaluations. She will likely have a major say in the assignment of your final grade.

Since it is difficult to telephone someone you do not know well in order to say nothing in particular, you might prefer to be proactive in establishing a relationship. If you take another class with her, the opportunity will arise in class. If she is not one of your classroom instructors, a word in the hallway might suffice, or a moment in her office when the door is open. You just want to ensure that there has been some contact between the two of you throughout your practicum.

Your Practicum Tutorial Teacher

Your practicum tutorial teacher will likely instruct you in a seminar format in the classroom at your school. This class is an opportunity to help integrate practice by organizing social work–related theory so that the practice and service you do in your practicum setting is logical and based on previous research findings and theory.

In this class, you will share your experiences and ideas with other students who will also be in their practicums. Some of your experiences will be like those of your classmates. Others may share very different situations they are facing in their practicum settings. All of these experiences related will add to your understanding of real-life social work practice. Many questions and situations in the classroom need to be held confidential. It is important for you to keep in mind that confidential means just that—confidential. Passing on confidential information while you are in your first practicum setting will guarantee that you will not have the opportunity to take a second: You will probably be asked to leave your practicum.

You, the Student

The most important influence in your practicum experience is undoubtedly you. You differ from other students in skills, personality, background, value systems, and learning style. Note that a learning style does not refer to what you have learned already. It refers to *how* you learn—to the way in which new material ideally should be presented to you so that you can absorb it most effectively. For example, if you want to acquire integrated assessment skills, you might read about interviewing, as well as approaches, methods, and empirically based literature about assessment methods and client responses; or, you could listen to someone tell you about interviewing, watch a videotape, practice a role-play, or participate in group discussions. Probably you will do all of these things, but one or two of them are more likely than the others to be more effective for and suited to you.

It is important to be aware of and understand how you learn best so you can maximize available learning situations for yourself during your practicum setting. Of course, you will learn in many different ways, and the fact that you learn best in one way does not mean that you cannot learn in all the other ways.

Nevertheless, if you know you learn well by reflective observation (watching), for example, you should find as many opportunities as you can to watch other people doing things. If you learn better by abstract conceptualization (thinking), you should spend more time reading and trying to fit the information you acquire into a conceptual framework that your can understand.

Your practicum instructor should understand your learning style as well. After all, she is going to be deciding on your learning assignments, particularly in the first few weeks when you are not yet ready to create your own learning opportunities. If she knows how you learn best, she will be more able to find assignments that will suit you. She will also be able to deliberately find assignments that do not appear to suit you in order to encourage you to learn in other ways.

It might be interesting to find out what your practicum instructor's learning style is. It would be a good idea to simply ask the question directly. However, be prepared if she does not know. People who learn best in one particular way and have always done so have a tendency to assume that other people learn the same way they do. Therefore, they teach the way they like to learn and may not have considered that there are other learning styles and complementary teaching methods.

Other Mapmakers

Other mapmakers in your practicum journey are other social work professionals, your classmates, and all the agencies in the community that interact with your specific agency and practicum setting. You may be supervised by one or more professionals in relation to some particular assignment. These professionals will then consult with your practicum instructor about your "overall" progress.

There should be no difficulty here as long as you are honest with all participants. Problems with another professional should be resolved directly with that individual if at all possible. You do not want to put anyone in a position where he or she is expected to take sides. Learning active collaboration is an important part of effective and professional social work practice.

MAPMAKING AND EFFECTIVE LEARNING

By now you have likely come to realize there are many things that influence your mapmaking ability and learning plans. In this final section, some of the more intangible aspects of effective learning are raised. Let us now take each one in turn, knowing full well that they may interact with one another.

Your Feelings

Most likely you are feeling excited and fearful about your first practicum experience—we know the four of us were. Excitement and fear can be motivating but, if there is an excess of either, you can become immobilized. You could be so excited that you are chomping at the bit to get started but you have not even figured out your practicum setting's intake form. Or you could be so scared of "damaging" someone that you keep postponing your first client interview or community meeting.

You can learn best when you feel energized and are not preoccupied with personal distractions and concerns. If your dog has died, your best friend has left the country, or a parent has become ill, you will probably not learn very much. If, for example, your social life, home life, and other classes take up so much of your time that you have little energy left to devote to learning within your practicum setting, this is definitely a moment for compromise. You need to take time to get some pleasure out of life and give yourself some rewards. On the other hand, maybe *one* of your leisure time activities could go, or you might consider dropping that extra class on multivariate statistics you thought you could handle.

Your Interests

You will learn best if you are interested in the content being taught to you. This will make it meaningful in your perception. The content has to be presented in a way that makes sense to you, which involves a number of factors. You need to be able to communicate to your practicum instructor the factors that help you make sense of the content being presented. For some students, difficult material should be presented more slowly and repeated more often than easier material. In other situations, not too much should be presented all at once. Repetition should incorporate different ways of teaching the same thing to make use of different learning styles. Material that can be presented in stages should be taught in a way that it builds from the simple to the complex, each stage related to the stage that went before it. Periodically, everything presented to date should be summarized.

Also, you need to see the relevance in what you are learning. You may not see, for example, why you need to know anything about the theory of organizations. You may plan to spend your career talking to Ms. Banks about the wisdom of institutionalizing her mother, without seeing how organizational theory will assist you in this endeavor. If it is not clear to you why you are being taught something, or why you are being instructed to do something, *ask*. Often a simple explanation will trigger a connection and motivate you to learn in an entirely new direction.

There is nothing difficult about this except actually doing it. For example, your practicum instructor may be quite prepared to present difficult material more slowly if she knows what you find difficult. And she will accommodate your learning style if she knows what it is. She will repeat what needs to be repeated and summarize what needs to be summarized, but she will not be able to do this without your active participation. Your practicum instructor is not a mind reader and you have to tell her exactly what your learning style is and how you learn best. It is important for you to remember also that she is there for your learning and that she wants you to learn as much as you can within the short amount of time you will have together.

Your Capabilities

Consider these three possibilities: your practicum instructor has overestimated your capabilities so that the tasks you are assigned are too difficult; you are never praised when you have done something well; or you are always praised even though you regularly make mistakes. You will learn best when your learning is followed by positive reinforcement.

However, if you find that you are unable to cope with so many assignments, you should say so. Social workers are taught to start where the client is; educators are taught to start where the student is; but your practicum instructor may not know where you are. She may be basing your assignments on faulty assumptions about your knowledge level and skills, not remembering that the social work student she had last semester was on his second practicum, while you are on your first.

If you are to learn anything at all in this situation, you will have to be candid about what you do not know and cannot do. Suggest that you work up to your impossible assignment by way of a number of easier assignments. Ask your practicum instructor and practicum liaison for help.

If you are never praised or recognized when you have done something well, there is always the possibility that you have not done as well as you thought. Perhaps your practicum instructor hesitates to give you negative feedback and is avoiding the issue by giving you no feedback at all. Again, the thing to do is to ask. Select some part of an assignment that you think you did particularly well and ask if you did it to an acceptable standard. In what ways did you not meet the expectation? How could it have been improved?

This approach might elicit a number of gentle criticisms that may surprise and dismay you. When you have thought about the concerns raised, you will have to consider not just that particular assignment but the whole relationship between you and your practicum instructor. Perhaps you do not respond well to negative feedback and have been sending nonverbal signals to that effect. Maybe she is sacrificing your learning for fear of injuring your self-esteem.

This is a matter that definitely needs to be discussed. If your practicum instructor does not initiate the discussion, then you will have to, perhaps by asking politely why she did not mention these negative aspects before. It is always possible, of course, that your accomplishments have been brilliant in every respect but your practicum instructor may consider the timing of "praise" to really be the critical element. If you are praised continually, even in situations where you have doubts about your performance, you will eventually lose faith in your practicum instructor's judgment. You might mention to her that you want to hear and discuss what she thinks you do not do well or where you made a mistake, not just the good stuff.

Your Desire to Get Going

After spending a number of days filling your unscheduled time with the exploration of your practicum setting, exploration of the local community that houses your practicum, and countless cups of coffee, you might start to get impatient. It may seem that you will never meet with your first group, never interview your first client, never do anything more constructive than hover in the wake of very busy social workers.

From your practicum instructor's point of view, this is a time of assessment. If you are to observe another worker's interviewing session, your practicum instructor has to be sure that the session and the worker chosen are appropriate to your learning objectives. If you are to see a client right away, your practicum instructor will likely have several in mind, with goals that appear to be obtainable within the time frame of your practicum setting.

Some clients are good at training social worker students because they have experience with "the system." They know what questions you ought to ask and obligingly answer them for you. They fill in awkward pauses, propose solutions to their own dilemmas, help you along when you falter in drawing a genogram, and generally guide you on your way.

Your practicum instructor has to find a client/consumer for you whose problems will not overwhelm you, one who will not be hurt by your inexperience, one who can help you reach your learning goals and, in turn, can be helped by you. This is not easy and it takes some time. If you are patient, however, a range of clients, client systems, and/or projects will appear and the results will be more positive than you ever imagined.

SUMMARY

Organizing your map for effective learning to take place requires thoughtful consideration of many factors. Creating a learning environment involves paying attention to the goals and objectives of your practicum setting and to the influences of others and their contributions. You define your goals and objectives when you write your learning agreement. They must be related to your practicum setting and to the achievement standards required by your social work program. To ensure that all your objectives will be met, examine your program's practicum evaluation form at the beginning of your practicum. You can then identify your learning goals and objectives and tailor them to the evaluation form.

With regard to yourself, creating a learning environment demands attention to the way you learn. Once you have evaluated your learning style, you can create opportunities that will enable you to learn most effectively. Learning in general may be enhanced if you are aware of both aspects influencing your learning and your respective learning styles. The power of planning cannot be underestimated.

We will now turn to the factors that affect the management of your practicum setting—the topic of the following chapter.

Name: _____

EXERCISE 4.1: SELF-ASSESSMENT AGENDA
FOR LEARNING GOALS

———————————————————

Type: Application

Purpose: To develop a learning agenda.

Exercise: Complete the sentences on the following page. They will direct your thinking about what you want to learn, and need to learn, as well as areas of strength and areas for further growth.

Notes on Use

———————————————————

Student: Be honest with yourself as you complete the sentences on the following page. Review them with your practicum instructor to help develop your learning agenda.

Practicum Instructor: Consider your student's responses to the sentence completion exercise. Offer your own perspective.

Practicum Tutorial Teacher: Ask students to share their completed sentences with each other.

✔ I am most concerned about learning:

✔ I am next most concerned about learning:

✔ I am particularly good at:

✔ I struggle with:

✔ I need to know more about:

✔ One thing others say I do very well is:

✔ One thing others say I need to work on is:

✔ I was recently challenged by:

Name: _____

EXERCISE 4.2: USER-ACTION STRATEGIES

Type: Application

Purpose: To understand what you need to do to realize your learning goals and that there are many different ways to accomplish learning goals.

Exercise: Brainstorming is an activity that is helpful when you need to generate many different alternatives to an issue. Identify something you would like to learn in your practicum, such as: to focus interviews, to know how to chair a meeting, to be more assertive in a group meeting, to help clients focus on strengths as opposed to problem behaviors, to document immediately after sessions or meetings, or to analyze video recordings in terms of your use of self. List ways that you can accomplish this learning. Which ways would work best for you?

Notes on Use

Student: This exercise will give you a chance to be creative and to understand that new ways of achieving a goal are possible. In other words, generating new ideas can help you overcome the tendency to view or think about a situation in just one way by opening up other possibilities. On the next page, identify a goal for change and the range of actions that you may take to accomplish it. Consider the degree of ease or difficulty you had and comment on which ideas are achievable and which you think are just too "wild" to be considered a possibility.

Practicum Instructor and *Practicum Tutorial Teacher:* Review your student's goal for change. Have students share with another student the feedback and quality of the proposed strategies. Have students note differences in the viability of the solutions. Provide any suggestions, additions, and comments. Ask students about their preferences regarding the formats they chose. Have them share the reasons and discuss. Students need to see that strategies should fit their resources, style, circumstances, and motivation level.

✔ Things I want to learn:

✔ Ways that I can take action to learn:

✔ Which of those actions fit best for me and my situation:

Name: _____

EXERCISE 4.3: UNDER THE MICROSCOPE

Type: Application

Purpose: To practice writing a learning goal.

Exercise: Write one learning goal so that it is meaningful, clear, simple, measurable, and challenging.

Notes on Use:

Student: Select one of things you want to learn in your practicum and, using the headings on the following page, develop it into a learning goal.

Practicum Instructor and *Practicum Tutorial Teacher:* Review your student's selected learning goal and provide helpful feedback and instructional advice.

✔ One learning goal I want to accomplish:

✔ Strategies for learning it:

✔ Who can help you achieve your goal?

✔ What resources do you need to achieve your goal?

✔ What is the time line for achieving your goal?

✔ What actions or strategies are the best fit for you?

✔ Is the goal meaningful for your learning experience?

✔ Is your goal stated clearly?

✔ Is your strategy to achieve the goal realistic and easy to implement?

✔ Is your goal measurable? How will you know when it is achieved?

✔ Are you challenging yourself to learn new ways with this goal?

Name: _____

EXERCISE 4.4: YOUR PRELIMINARY IMPRESSIONS OF YOUR PRACTICUM

Type: Reflection

Purpose: To obtain information and impressions of your initial integration into your practicum setting.

Exercise: On the following page, complete a preliminary self-assessment of your adjustment and beginning work in your practicum setting.

Notes on Use

Student: Comment on your initial adjustment to your practicum setting and initial work with various client systems. Add any other comments about the beginning phase of your practice in your practicum setting. This exercise should be completed around the third week of your practicum. After completing the following page, what are your general overall initial impressions of your practicum setting? This will provide you with some initial sense of how you are settling into your practicum setting.

Practicum Instructor: Discuss with your student the various ways of improving the practicum orientation process.

Practicum Tutorial Teacher: Have students share their different beginning practicum experiences as an opportunity for them to learn about different practicum settings.

✔ Describe the aspect of the orientation process that was most effective in your practicum setting:

✔ Describe your beginning work with client/consumer systems:

✔ Comment on whether you are able to use your preferred approaches to learning and what other approaches you would like to use:

Name: _____

EXERCISE 4.5: YOUR INSTRUCTOR'S PRELIMINARY IMPRESSIONS OF YOU

Type: Reflection

Purpose: To review the beginning phase of getting started from the perspective of your practicum instructor.

Exercise: On the following page, ask your practicum instructor to share her preliminary impression of your beginning work with assignments and adjustment to your practicum setting. This exercise can be completed around the end of the third week of your practicum.

Notes on Use

Student: Reflect on what your practicum instructor said about you and devise strategies to incorporate her comments into your practice.

Practicum Instructor: Identify any differences in perceptions regarding your student's initial adjustment to the practicum setting and your developing relationship. Identify strengths that can be used to manage any concerns.

Practicum Tutorial Teacher: Ask students to share their preliminary evaluations and give feedback to each other.

✔ Describe your student's adjustment to his or her practicum setting:

✔ Describe your student's emerging strengths:

✔ Note any emerging concerns you have about your student:

Name: _____

EXERCISE 4.6: EFFECTIVE LEARNING AND YOU

Type: Reflection

Purpose: To identify factors that may influence or affect your learning and achieving your goals.

Exercise: To identify factors that might influence or affect you in achieving your goals as written in your learning agreement.

Notes on Use

Student: Select one aspect about your practicum setting or your personal style that could influence or affect the achievement of effective learning and, on the following page, explore what this means to you based on your experience in your practicum. See if you can identify a particular incident or situation that will help you explore this.

Practicum Instructor and *Practicum Tutorial Teacher:* Review your students' learning agreements and ask about any factors that might influence or affect their achievement.

✔ After rereading my learning agreement I can see that one thing that might influence or affect my achievement is:

• Chapter Four •

✔ An incident or situation from my practicum:

✔ What this incident or situation means to me in relation to my learning:

✔ In summary, how do you feel you learn best in your practicum setting?
  Give specific examples.

Part Three

Performance Matters

P ART THREE CONTAINS THREE CHAPTERS that might be analogous to detailed road maps. Each one will help you navigate a different part of your journey. Chapter Five will assist you on the path you take with your practicum instructor. Chapter Six will direct you through the details of making sense of your day-to-day activities, via supervisory conferences. Chapter Seven will help you evaluate your chosen path as you go, so that you can make changes to your itinerary while you are en route to your destination—becoming a professional social worker.

Chapter Five

Learning by Supervision

MANAGING YOUR LEARNING BEFORE IT MANAGES YOU

I N ORDER TO TURN your *doing* into *learning*, you need to reflect critically on your performance within your practicum setting. Supervision is the process that enables you to do this. Educational supervision in your practicum setting is essential to your learning: It is where the being, knowing, thinking, and doing parts of becoming a social worker can be explored, developed, and enhanced.

Helping you examine what you currently know and are doing, who you are and your thoughts and feelings, will give you insight and understanding into what more you need to learn. This requires planning, organizing, coordinating, directing, controlling, and supervising various aspects of your performance within your practicum setting. We would like you to notice that you are starting to get heavily involved in your practicum learning experience and will now begin to manage your practicum experience rather than having it manage you.

If you are engaged in at least some of the planning, organizing, or coordinating functions, it may be said with fairness that you are managing your learning to some degree. The directing, controlling, and supervising parts of turning "your doing" into "your learning" are less clear since you are the one being supervised. It is fair to say that the quality of the supervision you receive in your practicum setting is directly related to your future performance as a professional social worker. Knowing what you can expect from your practicum instructor and from supervision is the first step in managing your learning.

What follows is our view of the "perfect" practicum instructor. This may be unfair, since perfection is good in theory but may not fit the reality of your situation. What we describe might be viewed as "super" supervision by the "perfect" practicum instructor—which assumes, of course, that you are the "model" student and that you and your practicum instructor have the "ideal" relationship.

As you have likely figured out by now, there are many factors that affect your practicum instructor's ability to be perfect, that prevent your supervision from being super, your performance from being model, and your relationship with your practicum instructor from being ideal. But if you can at least envision "best practices," then you will have a sense of direction.

THE PERFECT PRACTICUM INSTRUCTOR

The perfect practicum instructor is available to you, has a solid knowledge base, can direct your learning, and has fair expectations of you. These broad categories include being skillful at teaching and at practice, being willing to be observed and questioned, and being able to give support and establish a trusting and a safe environment. It also helps if the practicum instructor is clairvoyant, empowering, intuitive, insightful, nurturing, and fully engaged in her own process of becoming.

Is Available

Your expectations of your practicum instructor need to take into account that supervising you is likely in addition to all her other workplace responsibilities. Nonetheless, your ability to access your practicum instructor and her availability to you is a factor affecting the quality of your learning. How available is she for you? Does she schedule, and keep, regular supervisory conference meetings with you and are these sessions frequent enough and long enough to adequately monitor your progress? Is she there between supervisory conferences to give advice, support, and direction if you encounter the unexpected?

An important element of availability is approachability. Your practicum instructor may be physically there when you have a problem, but is she there in the sense that you are comfortable in asking your questions? Does she encourage contact or does she make you feel that you are a nuisance, a burden, an unwanted interruption? If you do feel like a nuisance, try to decide objectively whether you *are* a nuisance. Was your anxiety level so high at the beginning that you asked about *everything*, even things you could have figured out for yourself? Your perfect practicum instructor should be able to manage your dependence without injuring your self-esteem.

Has an Adequate Knowledge Base

The perfect practicum instructor has an up-to-date knowledge base that she can access according to the situation. She will know just about everything there is to know about the type of clients your agency and practicum setting serve as well as the local community resources, and she is able to transmit this knowledge to you in the best way at the most opportune time. There may be other areas, however, in which your knowledge is greater.

It is sometimes difficult for a practicum instructor to keep up with the pressures of her own work and also to keep abreast of innovations in the field. You as a student, newly emerged from your textbooks, are in a position to bring information into your setting about the latest social work theories and techniques. The pearls of wisdom provided to you by your classroom teachers can be shared with your practicum instructor and other agency staff. However, sharing these pearls is a matter requiring discretion, because your practicum instructor may feel threatened by you. She may feel that her own knowledge and skills are indirectly being questioned. Nevertheless, one of the hallmarks of a knowledgeable person is the willingness to acquire new knowledge.

Is your practicum instructor willing to consider new ideas and approaches? Is she receptive and not defensive and willing to admit, without embarrassment, that she does not know everything?

The perfect practicum instructor is able to broaden and deepen your knowledge. In addition to the knowledge you are acquiring about the types of clients your agency serves and the special problems that may confront them are you learning anything about management, about group process, about interpersonal relations? Perhaps your practicum instructor wants you to be on a research committee, or suggests that you go with her to an interdisciplinary meeting, or asks for your help with the budget. Perhaps she wants you to design a newsletter using a graphics software program. These types of activities not only increase your knowledge but are a part of the way your perfect practicum instructor directs your learning.

Directs Your Learning

Your practicum instructor's ability to direct your learning is a critical factor to consider. Does she work with you on understanding your learning goals and objectives? Does she then assign you to projects relevant to those objectives and to clients or others who would challenge but not overwhelm you? Does she suggest added activities to expand your indirect learning such as sitting in on a committee meeting or paying a visit to a different community setting? Is the focus of your learning directed only to case management and agency-specific procedures, or does she link theory and practice to events and the dynamics of your assignments? Your practicum instructor's ability to help you integrate "classroom theoretical material" and "practicum practice" is a very important aspect of your total social work learning experience.

You are expected to take primary responsibility for your learning experience but your practicum instructor is supposed to guide you, especially at the beginning. The perfect practicum instructor is able to select cases, tasks, and projects with regard to their level of difficulty and your current skill level. If you are bored or in over your head, your practicum instructor may have made a misjudgment.

Regardless of how perfect your practicum instructor may be in directing your learning, she is not a mind reader. Inasmuch as there will be situations where the work is too difficult, too easy, or just about right, you might discuss these so she will then have a better idea of which assignments are appropriate. Does your practicum instructor help you understand your own habitual patterns or themes of interaction? Does she point out your emerging interviewing styles? Does she create links for you between what you did and what you might have done in a way that enables you to do it better next time?

As a beginning social work student, it is likely that you have a natural affinity for people. On the other hand, the stress of conducting a first interview, you may remember little of what you were taught in school. Theories about engaging and focusing, active listening, and summarizing may be lost in the general confusion. Nevertheless, your natural talents will carry you through. Empathy and warmth may be instinctive for you; interest may be genuine; caring may be easy. It is your practicum instructor's task to mold this natural ability into a conscious technique. She must make you aware of your strengths so that you can use them purposefully to benefit your clients.

For example, she may have asked you to videotape your first interview or to make a process recording. She may have then pointed out to you that you were using the interviewing skill called "reflection of content" when you repeated to Ms. Smith something she had just said. When you rephrased Ms. Smith's words to give them a slightly different meaning, you were using "interpretation." The silence you were worried about in the middle of the interview was, in fact, a "positive use of silence." One of your questions resulted in "clarification"; another was an "appropriate use of confrontation"; a third was an "inappropriate change of topic," which allowed your client to evade the issue at hand.

Through this kind of analysis, your practicum instructor can help you to be aware of the interviewing techniques you may have used by chance. Her comments are specific and constructive. Her criticisms are directed at your practice, your struggle to become a professional social worker, and not at you personally. She is able to use your initial efforts as a teaching tool to reinforce your strengths and point to areas that need improvement. These, then, are some of the ways your practicum instructor can direct your learning.

Has Realistic Expectations of You

The perfect practicum instructor has realistic and fair expectations. She does not expect too much of you or too little, and her expectations are similar to your own. One of the problems facing you as a beginning practicum student is that you are usually not sure what the expectations are. A problem facing the social work profession is that there is little agreement about what the expectations ought to be. For example, everyone agrees that you should be able to *"identify and select appropriate helping strategies."* However, the *degree* to which you should be able to identify and select appropriate helping strategies by the end of your first practicum is open to question.

You will probably conclude that your practicum instructor's expectations are too high if you find difficulty in meeting them, too low if you meet them very easily, and about right if they give you a satisfying challenge. You might also compare her standards with the standards imposed on other students by other practicum instructors.

SUPER SUPERVISION

Your scheduled supervisory conferences with your practicum instructor are fundamental to your learning. Therefore, you need to plan your supervisory conferences in the same way you plan for the rest of your practicum. What will be the particular focus of this supervisory conference? What do you hope to achieve in it? What do you need to have prepared to realize your expectations? What similar or different expectations might your practicum instructor have?

Educational supervision is a special type. There are components to it that make it different from others, such as staff supervision, and practical factors that need to be negotiated and understood. Educational supervision is most typically done one-on-one between you and your practicum instructor, but group supervision is a widely accepted variation. For your supervision to truly be "super," a number of seemingly opposing forces need to be balanced in a way that respects you, your learning style, and your learning needs—and the balance must suit your practicum instructor.

Components of Super Supervision

There are three essential components of educational supervision that are affected by practical factors. Supervisory conferences should include each component in every session, however, they may occupy varying amounts of time and emphases depending on the focus for the particular supervisory conference. The various components are: feedback on your performance, case/project analysis, and personal/professional issues.

Feedback on Your Performance

Evaluation is an ongoing process; it begins on the first day and continues with every contact between you and your practicum instructor. Its purpose is to provide you with timely and specific feedback so that you can use each learning experience as a stepping-stone to the next.

In order for feedback to be useful to you it needs to be: timely—is given soon after the event; clear—is stated directly in language that is meaningful to you; balanced—includes both your strengths and limitations, the positives and negatives; useful—helps you examine alternatives and options; relevant—relates to a specific event, incident, or action; and, reciprocal—invites your comments and perspective on the feedback. To enhance the quality of the feedback that is given to you it may be necessary to prompt your practicum instructor using the above characteristics as a guide.

For example, a remark that "your interviewing skills need work" is obviously true: Everyone's interviewing skills need work, but it is not a particularly helpful evaluative comment. To be helpful, it has to be specific and suggest remedial action. For example, "Pat has difficulty exploring the client's meaning on an issue" points to a clearly defined interviewing skill that needs improvement. The remedy could easily be expressed as, "Pat needs to ask clients more frequently to give examples of specific situations to clarify meaning."

The perfect practicum instructor gives feedback in a way that helps you develop. She is sensitive to your ego but not overprotective. She says what needs to be said in a way that you can hear it and do something about it.

Case and Project Analyses

This involves an examination of one of your cases (or projects) from multiple perspectives. It is more than reviewing the procedures and activities you have undertaken, although this is part of it. The analysis should help you draw upon knowledge and make connections with other experiences so that you can transform doing into learning. It should help you consider the implications of the context, ethical issues, and diversity variables in understanding the outcome and effectiveness of your work. To facilitate this analysis you may need to ask your practicum instructor for her opinions and perspectives, again prompting for this type of information when needed. Activities that encourage you to reflect on your work, such as process recordings or interview skill checklists, are helpful in the analysis.

Personal and Professional Issues

Understanding personal and professional issues helps you sort out your emotional reactions to clients or situations and any value conflicts that may have arisen. It should provide an opportunity for you to discuss your impact on your practicum setting and others in your agency. Most importantly there should be an opportunity for you and your practicum instructor to discuss the relationship between the two of you, how it is evolving, and the impact of your differences such as age, gender, ethnicity, and race.

You should also know how the relationship you have with your practicum instructor is affecting your ability to learn. For example, does the fact that she evaluates you, and either determines or recommends that you pass, leave you feeling too powerless to disagree with her or assert yourself? It is much easier to discuss the other two components (i.e., your reactions to clients and your effect on the organization) because it is "out there." But putting your thoughts about you and your practicum instructor ("How it is going between the two of you?") on the table will result in a powerful, purposeful, and productive learning exchange.

Practical Factors

Practical factors related to your supervisory conferences are largely concerned with what, when, and how: *What* are you going to talk about, *when* are you going to talk about it, and *how* can you facilitate the discussion. In all probability, the *when* will arise on a regular basis—from 2:00 to 3:00 PM on Friday afternoons, for example. Occasionally, the Friday supervisory conference will be switched to Wednesday, or you may skip a week or schedule an extra conference to meet a particular need. *When* is not at all important so long as both you and your practicum instructor *know* when, because both of you need to be prepared.

The *what* part is a different matter. Of course, you will know in advance of the supervisory conference that you want to discuss Ms. Taylor's refusal to tell you her *real* problem. You will probably have to let your practicum instructor have Ms. Taylor's file and a videotape or a process recording of your last interview with her. You will have to formulate some tentative hunches about where you think the *real* problem lies and why you think she is avoiding the *real* issue. You will have to be prepared to discuss which interviewing techniques learned in your interviewing skills course you used to elicit the information and why you feel they were unsuccessful. You will have to be ready with suggestions as to what you will say to Ms. Taylor next time and why you think this different approach might prove to be more effective than the previous ones.

All this will be in vain if your practicum instructor wants to discuss your weekly time sheet instead. Accordingly, you must come to an agreement with her about the focus of the supervisory conference *before* it starts. If you cannot plan for next week at the end of this week's supervisory conference, you should schedule five minutes during the week to decide whether the agenda will be Ms. Taylor or time sheets. A brief written agenda will keep both of you focused. If it is to be Ms. Taylor, your practicum instructor will then have the opportunity to reread her file. If it is to be time sheets, you will have a chance to reflect over where you may have gone wrong.

You might also find that *when* is intimately connected with *what*. Your disappointment over the time sheets might occupy a brief five minutes; Ms. Taylor, on the other hand, might take ten times as long. You should therefore ensure that you and your practicum instructor have enough time available for the topics you have to discuss. If there is not enough time, ask for extra time in advance of the supervisory conference, or divide the material into two or three conferences, or select just the most important points.

How may also affect *when* and is definitely connected to *what*. For example, the resolution of Ms Taylor's distressing obstinacy may involve letting your practicum instructor watch your videotaped interview with her. To do this, you have to have the equipment available. The video may only be available for a certain time and in a certain place so you may have to make the necessary booking arrangements.

In addition, remember that a half-hour tape will take about ten times as long to view and discuss, so either you will need extra time or you will have to choose the vital parts in advance. By the time you have done all this, you will have acquired considerable expertise in the negotiating, organizing, and coordinating aspects of practicum management.

Group Supervision

Group supervision is a variation of the more typical and traditional type of one-to-one supervision. So far, the components and practical factors affecting your educational supervision have been discussed as though the individual supervisory conference is the only form of supervision that exists. Group supervision is a very important part of your practicum experience as well.

If you are placed separately from your classmates, particularly if you are located in a different department, group supervisory conferences may be one of the few opportunities you have to meet with them and find out what they are doing. Group supervisory conferences enable you to see your classmates' individual problem-solving approaches and, inevitably, you will be able to compare their experiences with your own. You can learn a lot so long as you remember that you are not in competition with one another. Their approaches may be different from yours but "different" does not mean better or worse.

Group supervision allows a wider selection of learning experiences to be undertaken. For example, a film is far more useful if you watch it and discuss it afterwards with someone else. Lectures and presentations are normally provided only to groups; even role-plays can be more effective if there are a number of participants, each watching and trying to improve on the performance of the others.

Some students need group supervisory conferences to develop a sense of professional identity. On the other hand, some students learn better in group settings. Some are not able to question the practicum instructor without the feeling of moral support and safety provided by other students. If at all possible, individual supervisory conferences should be balanced with group supervisory conferences.

The Balancing Act in Super Supervision

As we said earlier, there is a delicate balancing act in educational supervision that will affect the quality of your supervisory experience. If your learning is activated during supervisory conferences it is likely that there will be *productive tension* between you and your practicum instructor. These tensions are created by the dynamics inherent in the teaching and learning process and result from the attempts to find a balance in some of the opposing forces below:

✔ challenge versus support

✔ risk-taking versus safety

✔ demand for work versus self-directedness

✔ autonomy versus dependency

✔ authority versus mutuality

✔ learning objectives versus practicum setting's objectives

✔ education versus training

Your practicum setting should provide you with an excellent opportunity to question your underlying beliefs and assumptions about the world of "social work." This process needs to be triggered, however. It can be facilitated by your practicum instructor, who may need to *challenge* you to explore alternative ways of being, thinking, feeling, and acting. But your instructor needs to *support* you in your struggle to make sense of things and in leaving the old ways behind, which can be a wrenching experience.

Challenge is central to helping you think critically. It prompts self-scrutiny, consideration of alternatives, and the taking of action. But it is not the same as abuse or denigration and it is not a license to insult you or for attacking your self-esteem. However, challenging assumptions can be somewhat threatening and intimidating, so it is essential that your practicum instructor provide you with a healthy measure of support and is sensitive to the amount of challenge that you can tolerate.

The ability to challenge you without intimidating or threatening you is one of the most difficult skills for your practicum instructor to develop. You may need some patience and understanding if she is new and still learning how to do this because it is somewhat of an art to know when to challenge and when to support.

Too much challenge can overload you and undermine your self-esteem, but not enough challenge may create a warmly satisfying relationship in which you learn nothing.

To integrate new ways of being, thinking, knowing, and acting involves *taking risks* in trying new things but also requires *safety* so that you have the permission and comfort you need to transform your attitudes and assumptions. Through this process you will acquire a more inclusive, flexible view of the world—ranging from fixed rules that apply in all circumstances to contextually sensitive applications, depending on the circumstances.

Your practicum instructor has to find a balance that suits you between giving you work, tasks, and assignments (i.e., *demanding work)* and allowing you to direct your energies and take initiative in terms of the work, tasks, and assignments you take on (i.e., *self-directedness*).

Sometimes tensions can arise in relation to the degree of *autonomy* or freedom you are given to make choices and how *dependent* you are upon your practicum instructor for direction and affirmation. Another type of tension is related to how you and your practicum instructor address the power differential in terms of her *authority* over you (e.g., making judgments about your progress and performance) and the degree of *mutuality* attained (e.g., collaborating and agreeing upon assignments and expectations). Just the fact that you are *only* a student can, at times, be disempowering. If your practicum setting is quite hierarchical in structure this might also reinforce that your place is at the bottom of the pecking order. Feeling powerless is not conducive to learning. However, neither is it useful to deny the existence of the authority or the power differential. Discussing the impact that your practicum instructor's authority and power have on you is an important step in finding the best balance for you.

Your practicum instructor may be under a great deal of pressure to get her work done. Therefore, she may experience pressure between meeting the *services goals* of your practicum setting (and agency for that matter), while also complying with your *educational objectives* to ensure that your learning experiences match your program's requirements. This is related to the final source of tension, which is the balance between *training* you for a specific job-related task and *educating* you for professional social work practice (i.e., knowledge and skills that are transferable from your practicum setting to the "real world").

As you can see, your practicum instructor has a lot to balance in trying to provide you with the kind of educational supervision that will meet your needs, your program's requirements, and your practicum setting's expectations. You can help her by being as clear and direct as you can in expressing yourself—what you are going through and what will be helpful to your learning, as this will lead to the ideal relationship.

THE IDEAL RELATIONSHIP

It is an accepted premise in social work education that having an "ideal" relationship with your practicum instructor is an enabling factor in your learning and plays an important part in the development of your attitudes, values, and professional identity. Therefore, it must be continually kept in mind that your ability to risk yourself in disclosing, documenting, and in being observed will be largely dependent on the relationship you have with her.

Your ability to step back and take a critical look at your work is affected by the relationship between the two of you. This relationship can be affected by a number of factors: differing expectations and attitudes due to differences in ethnic, cultural, or religious backgrounds; differences in age; differences in gender; and difficulties due to physical challenges. It is also affected by your learning style, communication pattern, and the way "authority issues" are dealt with and handled.

It goes without saying that the more you can be open and honest, share your feelings and thoughts, and communicate your struggles both with the work and with your relationship, the more fruitful will be your learning experience. The ideal relationship with your practicum instructor will enrich your learning but if you do not have or cannot develop this relationship, do not despair; you can still learn a great deal from the practicum. There are things you can do, however, to bring clarity to your sense of being different and to manage the differences between the two of you.

Sense of Being Different

Communicating about difference in any interaction is not an easy task. The discussion of cultural differences (including race, ethnicity, class, sexual orientation, etc.) is provocative, sensitive, controversial, and taboo. Failure to address your sense of being different can have damaging consequences for building the ideal relationship and proceeding with super supervision, just as it can interfere with your ability to establish a trusting client-worker helping process. Fear may cause an unwillingness to be open to new ways of understanding yourself in relation to others especially in the multicultural aspects of your identity.

As a student social worker you are required to know as thoroughly as possible the sense of being different as it relates to the lives of those you serve. You need to understand about oppression and discrimination. You need to understand about stereotyping and prejudice. You need to understand about bigotry and hatred. And what is difficult is that you need to understand these things in a very personal way. In doing so, you need to become increasingly aware of your own cultural background (and baggage); values, beliefs and traditions; ways these values, beliefs, and traditions are different from those of others; and how adherence to these may lead you to see others (those who don't adhere) as "less than," or "not as good as," or in need of "salvation," "conversion," or help in "finding *the* way."

Unless you make a conscious effort to value and appreciate them, these fundamental differences will create barriers to effective practice, supervision and learning. You need to explore how your thinking, knowing, being, and doing might vary as a result of racial, ethnic, class, and other cultural differences. The same barriers to developing the client-worker relationship may also impede the student-practicum instructor relationship. If you are older than your client, you may be deferred to because of your age; if younger, you may be rejected as a helper. If you are a woman with a male client, you may realize that from his perspective you have no status.

Managing Differences and Similarities

Your ability to honestly acknowledge the factors of difference and similarity between yourself, your practicum instructor, your clients, and others is critical to a productive term in your practicum. Relationships can be affected by a number of diversity factors such as: varying expectations and attitudes due to differences in ethnic, cultural, or religious backgrounds; differences in age, gender, and sexual orientation; or the presence of disabilities. Also affecting relationships are differences and similarities in learning style, communication patterns, and responses to power and authority. Certain differences and similarities present particular dilemmas that can be managed with planning and forethought.

There are likely to be differences and similarities in ethnic, cultural, and racial backgrounds. For example, you and your practicum instructor may both be from the mainstream group; or you may both be members of the same nonmainstream group; or you may be members of different nonmainstream groups; or you may be from the mainstream and your practicum instructor is not; or your practicum instructor may be mainstream and you are not. There can be differences and similarities in several areas or just a few.

When you and your practicum instructor are both mainstream, then you must pay particular attention to the requirements of ethnic-sensitive, cross-cultural objectives to ensure they are addressed.

If both of you are of the same nonmainstream background, the common heritage may create feelings of familiarity and speed up the formation of trusting relationship. Your practicum instructor may be able to anticipate the kinds of dilemmas or difficulties you may encounter and be able to prepare you to face these effectively. She may also make special allowances for you based on her own knowledge and experience or, alternatively, may demand a higher-than-usual level of performance. Expectations that are too high or too low can compromise learning. In some instances, being of the same nonmainstream group may cause either you or your practicum instructor to make poor choices based on faulty assumptions of sameness without considering intragroup differences.

If both of you come from nonmainstream but different groups, you will share the bond of being nonmainstream. Your practicum instructor will be attuned to the subtle manifestations of discrimination and will likely be more sensitive and aware of your struggles. On the other hand, your practicum instructor might have difficulty identifying culture-specific behaviors and attitudes that impact the teaching-learning exchange and will need to be vigilant in communicating about them.

If your practicum instructor is a person of color and you are white, your practicum instructor needs to open the dialogue regarding the difference, otherwise you may be tempted to ignore it. Your practicum instructor needs to take the lead. As a student, you may not know how and may be immobilized for fear of appearing racist; or you may indeed be color-blind, using "liberal, politically correct" thinking that color should not make a difference.

As a nonmainstream student you may have real difficulties when you work with the mainstream culture. There are the discriminatory slights and rejections that occur on a regular basis, which make it difficult for you to play a full part in the professional community. There is the possibility of racist attitudes and behaviors from clients. There is the risk of being seen as the "race expert" in the agency, especially if you are the only person of color or of a particular ethnic group. As such you are seen to be the most knowledgeable and asked for "the answers" on how best to work with or solve the problems of a particular group. If you are a nonmainstream student, it is not a fair expectation of you to train the other staff or have all the nonmainstream clients and assignments referred to you.

On the other hand, a student of color brings a level of knowledge and experience to the setting that needs to be acknowledged, seen as a strength and built upon, but not exploited. This requires the ability of the practicum instructor to negotiate and balance your learning needs with agency strengths. Your practicum instructor must be able to identify how a student of color can enrich the setting, validating your prior experience and expertise, while at the same time respecting your need to be a learner and not have your needs or requirements compromised. The success of this balancing act depends on your practicum instructor and student relationship.

Then, there is the matter of differing value systems. For example, one of the aims of this book is to motivate social work students to be proactive rather than reactive; that is, we believe you are supposed to take a primary role in setting your learning goals and objectives, suggesting appropriate assignments, organizing activities, and resolving conflicts. These many responsibilities, in turn, necessarily involve a certain attitude toward authority. If you have been taught that persons in authority should rarely be questioned and never be challenged, you may have difficulty in disagreeing with your practicum instructor. On the other hand, if you have been taught that admitting to a problem will cause you to lose face, you will be more likely to pretend that all is well.

It is quite essential that you be aware of these conflicts between your own values and the values of the mainstream, but such awareness may not help you very much. You may *know* that frankness in expressing your problems is held to be a virtue; however, you may not really *feel* that it is a virtue or even that it *ought* to be considered as such. Should you then try to change your beliefs to fit the mainstream values? If your effort is successful, to what degree have you betrayed your own culture? To what degree have you abandoned what may be still the *truth*?

Such questions can only be answered on a personal level by the individual concerned. Ideally, your practicum instructor will be sensitive to these issues, and will be ready to explore them with you when you are ready and able.

If you are a member of a minority group working with clients from your own culture, you may understand your clients better than your practicum instructor does. This can be threatening to her as she may perceive herself to be without a teaching role and may find out that her own helping interventions may be ineffective. In fact, she has a dual role: to learn the ways of your community and culture and to teach you to analyze your helping techniques and develop new ones. If you can interchange your own respective roles as teacher and learner, the two of you together can make a real contribution to the ethnic community and the social work profession. But this requires the ability to negotiate and balance your learning needs with the level of cultural competence of your practicum instructor and of your practicum setting in general.

Managing Differences in Gender

Gender differences between the student and practicum instructor may lead to reduced or heightened expectations about student performance. North America is a society in which male and female roles are in a state of transition. Men who open doors for women are not sure whether they are being patronizing or considerate; women who pour coffee for men are not sure whether they are being helpful or being subservient. Most of these dilemmas can be resolved by using common sense. The person who reaches the door first opens it; the person who is nearest to the pot pours the coffee.

Attitudes that are gender related may also be problematic. For example, a male practicum instructor may expect less from a female student than he would from a male student. He may expect her to be good with children even though she has no experience with them. He may defend and protect her when she needs to learn to defend and protect herself.

In the same way, a female practicum instructor with a male student may feel uncertain about her authority. She may adopt an overly authoritarian or passive attitude, either of which will interfere with the student-practicum instructor exchange. A seasoned practicum instructor will be aware of these potential traps, will be able to avoid them, and will help you to avoid them. Nevertheless, awareness on your part is essential if you are to establish and maintain a positive learning relationship.

Managing Differences in Age

Students, by tradition, are thought of as young. They are generally thought to be younger than the people who teach them. If you are a mature student, you are not alone; older social work students are becoming more common. Nevertheless, age has its associated problems and it needs to be acknowledged.

Mature Students

To begin with, if you are a mature student you are trying to form peer relationships with your classmates who, in some cases, may be younger than your children. The relationships you form may be cordial and supportive, but the quality of the support is rarely the same as it would have been with same-age peers.

It may have been a long time since you were last in school. You may wonder if your brain cells are still intact, if your classmates will laugh at your efforts, if your professors will laugh, or—worse yet—if they will all treat you with the patient, patronizing kindness which is only inappropriately afforded to the very old. A particular nemesis is often the computer. Younger social work students may have little affection for computers but at least they have met them before, if only through video games. Older students who did not have the opportunity to take typing classes in high school have more of a tendency to regard the computer as a dangerous and alien beast. The very fact that you are back in school means you are ready to *learn* new things. It is only a matter of combining this positive attitude with a willingness to ask for help when you find you do not understand.

Sometimes, asking for help is difficult for older students. Grey hairs, although they have nothing to do with wisdom, are certainly supposed to indicate experience. Your clients, and other professionals alike, may show surprise when you introduce yourself as a social work student. You may even read on Mr. Robert's face that if you are *still* a social work student at your age, he has little hope in solving the authority conflict he is having with his children.

All this can be especially difficult if you have recently changed careers. You were probably competent in the job you had before, but in this new field you may believe you have lost your accustomed sense of usefulness and worth. Not only may you *feel* useless, you are obliged to submit your perceived "uselessness" to the scrutiny of your practicum instructor.

It is up to your practicum instructor to point out to you that your experience *does* count. If your prior experience was in a related field, you should be able to use parts of it to shed light on some aspects of your new work, perhaps on the social problems faced by your practicum setting. If your experience is unrelated, it is still experience. Your previous experience has likely taught you how to interact with people, has given you emotional maturity, and has provided you with a long-term perspective on the purposes of learning.

Some difficulties may arise if your experience has been in an area where self-determination is less important than control. For example, nurses usually do not discuss with patients the advisability of taking medication. Teachers usually do not debate with students the wisdom of attending school. If you have been accustomed to making decisions *for* people, it might be hard for you to let your clients make them on their own, particularly if you disagree with the decisions they make. It should be noted that you should always discuss your dilemmas with your practicum instructor, your practicum liaison, or your practicum tutorial teacher.

The specific person to approach should be guided by logic and availability. However, a word of caution. Always try to work things out with your practicum instructor before you approach your practicum liaison or practicum tutorial teacher. It is important for you to know what their various roles are before you approach anyone.

When the Student Is Older Than the Instructor...

The practicum instructor–student relationship may be difficult if you are older than she is. She may feel uncomfortable acting as teacher and you may feel just as uncomfortable in the role of student. Probably, your instructor will take the initiative in discussing the age matter with you as a preliminary to exploring your other feelings about your new student role. If she does not, it is up to you to make it clear that in this particular setting *you* are the social work student and *she* is the practicum instructor. You accept that; you expect that on the basis of this understanding she will share with you her greater knowledge of social work and you will share with her your wider experience of life in other fields.

If you have worked in the social work field before, you may present your practicum instructor with an even greater challenge. You may feel that you are as competent as she is and resent her instruction. On the other hand, you may play down your experience because you would like to be just another social work student, the same as everybody else. Either of these attitudes will lead you to disaster. A student may have worked, yet not put the knowledge later learned in the classroom into action. Without realizing it, many people continue to do the wrong thing for years.

Work experience, even in social work or in a related field, does not necessarily put a student ahead of one without that experience. The most sensible thing to do is to ask your practicum instructor's help in deciding what you know, what you do not know, and how you can best fill in the gaps. You may begin at a higher level than the other students, but the process of setting learning goals and objectives, doing activities to meet the objectives, and analyzing failures will remain the same. For you, challenging yourself is surely one of your personal learning goals.

Managing Differences Due to Physical Challenges

If you are disabled, you may present a special situation for both your practicum setting and your social work program. The most common physical problems include motor disabilities, which may necessitate a wheelchair, and hearing or vision impairments ranging from moderate to profound deafness or blindness. Most educational institutions are now making arrangements to allow students with motor disabilities to move around the campuses and have access to most classrooms. Special assistance in the form of readers, attendants, interpreters, Braille texts, and special electronic equipment has made it possible for students with hearing or vision impairments to keep up with classroom work.

A practicum setting, however, is a different matter. Students with disabilities face the community daily and are well aware of what they need to function, but facing the community as a private individual and facing it as a beginning social work student are very different things. To begin with, there is the matter of access. Public buildings are increasingly being made accessible to those with a physical disability, but there are still smaller practicum settings with offices that can only be reached by circumventing obstacles in the hallway and climbing up three flights of stairs.

One answer to this, of course, is for you to obtain a practicum setting in a rehabilitation agency. Facilities will be on hand since you will be working with clients who have disabilities. You will have the opportunity to begin your professional life with colleagues and members of the public who are accustomed to interacting with people who are physically challenged. You may be more comfortable, your colleagues may be more comfortable, and your personal experience may be invaluable to your clients.

Some social work educators and students with disabilities feel strongly that a practicum in a rehabilitation setting is not an answer at all. Instead, they feel it is a statement that people who are physically disabled should work only with other people who are disabled because they cannot function anywhere else. This is a value question that you must decide for yourself. Given the limitations of stairs and cluttered hallways, you have the same opportunity as any other student to decide what you want from your practicum and what you do not want.

Next is the question of acceptance. Acceptance by agency staff and other professionals is vital to all social work students but, for the student with disabilities, it is critical. There are still many people, including a few social workers, who are unable to see past the physical disability to the person. They have a vague notion that because the legs no longer function, the brain must be affected too. In most cases, such fears can be avoided by a frank discussion with agency staff about the nature of the disability, the limitations imposed by the disability, the accommodations that need to be made, and the many things you are able to do despite the disability. Normally this discussion will take place before you arrive at the practicum setting and, for it to be useful, your practicum liaison should have your permission to discuss your physical disability with your practicum instructor and other staff.

None of these problems are insurmountable. Indeed, when the initial barriers have been overcome, you may find that your disability enables you to interact with your clients more readily. People with disabilities are less likely than others to be perceived as threatening. Your coping and problem-solving skills are probably well developed, and you may be able to engender a hopefulness in your clients.

On the other hand, it is possible that your practicum instructor and other colleagues will make allowances for you in ways that may endanger your learning. For example, lateness in completing an assignment may be tolerated on the grounds that you cannot walk. Sometimes, this is reasonable. You may indeed be late because it took you longer to get from one place to another. At other times, however, the task from which you are being excused may bear no relation whatsoever to your disability.

Such situations should not occur if you have discussed with your practicum instructor the precise nature of your disability and have agreed with her about the accommodations that may have to be made. The learning requirements of your social work program and the expectations of your practicum setting must be met whether you are disabled or not. It is up to you and your practicum instructor together to see that they are met by setting realistic learning goals and objectives and ensuring that any allowances made are specific only to your disability. If your practicum instructor has underestimated your coping skills, you should point out your capabilities, emphasizing that your disability is one factor in your life and not the whole of it.

SUMMARY

Turning doing into learning occurs through educational supervision and is affected by your relationship with your practicum instructor. Managing your learning means that you accept responsibility for defining and achieving your goals and objectives; suggesting, organizing, and documenting your activities; and participating actively in the supervisory process. Effective educational supervision depends on both practical and relationship factors. The practical factors involve arranging a time and place for supervision, agreeing on the supervisory conference topic in advance, gathering all available information about it, and ensuring that adequate time is allowed to discuss it. Relationship factors may be affected by differences in expectations and attitudes due to different ethnic or religious backgrounds, differences in age, differences in gender, and difficulties due to a physical disability.

Name: _____

EXERCISE 5.1: YOUR CULTURAL UNIQUENESS

Type: Reflective

Purpose: To understand the role that culture plays in your development as a professional social worker.

Exercise: Write a short (250 words) personal cultural autobiography using the outline provided on the following page. Since some of this information is very personal, you will need to judge what you are comfortable in sharing with others. Discuss this with your practicum instructor during your next supervision conference by focusing on differences and similarities.

Notes on Use

Student: Briefly describe your family of origin including information on family structure, cultural identity, racial and ethnic background, your neighborhood, and any other important factors you feel are important. Be prepared to discuss your cultural background with your practicum instructor. This may be difficult at first but will become easier as time goes on.

Practicum Instructor: Discuss the cultural autobiography of your student. Remember that some of this information may be personal in nature and should be treated as such. Based on your discussion, is there anything about your student's cultural background that will facilitate and or hinder providing services to clients who come from different backgrounds than the students?

Practicum Tutorial Teacher: Have students bring completed assignments to class for group discussion. Have the group discuss sociocultural factors that are important for them to consider in providing services to families. Discuss historical factors, discrimination issues, current problems, and future approaches. Debrief your students.

✔ Your Cultural Autobiography Outline

   ✔ Describe your family of origin
      - racial and ethnic background
      - religious affiliation
      - political leanings
      - socioeconomic status

   ✔ What were some of the things you learned in childhood about people who were from a different racial or ethnic group? About persons with disabilities? About those whose sexual orientation is different from yours? About poor people?

   ✔ What messages did you get about the roles of women and men, and the place of children from your family of origin?

   ✔ Who were defined as "outsiders" and "insiders" by your family? How were "outsiders" regarded and treated?

   ✔ Identify some of the biases, prejudices, and stereotypes you learned from your family of origin. Select one and describe how you became aware of its impact on your life or how you transformed it into a new way of thinking and behaving.

Name: _____

EXERCISE 5.2: MANAGING YOUR SUPERVISION

Type: Reflective

Purpose: You can evaluate the quality of your educational supervision and in doing so you can be clearer and perhaps more direct with your practicum instructor regarding the ways in which its quality can be enhanced.

Exercise: Read each item on the following three pages and think about your educational supervision. Then provide a rating for each item and write this in the blank space provided, where 1 means "very unsatisfactory" and 5 means "very satisfactory." More importantly, identify ways the rating can be improved.

Notes on Use

Student and *Practicum Instructor:* Independent of each other, complete your own assessment of the supervision items, the ratings, and the ways to improve them. Then, in your next supervisory conference, compare each item and discuss your various perspectives. Be candid, sincere, forthright, frank, and to the point. Do not fudge around.

Practicum Tutorial Teacher: Have students bring completed assignments to your class for group discussion. You can do two tasks with the class: (1) generate a list of ideas to improve each item and have your class pick the best suggestions, and (2) have your students role-play in pairs to practice introducing the issues in their future supervisory conferences. Debrief your students.

✔ I am able to participate in setting the purpose and agenda of the supervisory conference.
- Student's rating _____
What action needs to be taken to improve the rating?

✔ I come prepared with a specific and meaningful agenda.
- Student's rating _____
What action needs to be taken to improve the rating?

✔ I am able to stay focused on my agenda and learning needs.
- Student's rating _____
What action needs to be taken to improve the rating?

✔ I am able to present and discuss various ideas and feelings easily in supervision.
- Student's rating _____
What action needs to be taken to improve the rating?

✔ I am able to appropriately have alternative points of view without jeopardizing the practicum instructor relationship.
- Student's rating _____
What action needs to be taken to improve the rating?

✔ I am comfortable in giving and receiving feedback — in stating both positive and negative comments and concerns.
- Student's rating _____
What action needs to be taken to improve the rating?

✔ I can identify new ways for me to improve my practice.
  • Student's rating _____
    What action needs to be taken to improve the rating?

✔ I am able to address the effects of difference or similarity in my supervisor (e.g., race, culture, gender, age, ethnicity).
  • Student's rating _____
    What action needs to be taken to improve the rating?

✔ I am able to understand my learning style and how it influences my approach to learning.
  • Student's rating_____
    What action needs to be taken to improve the rating?

✔ I am giving the most to my supervision conference.
  • Student's rating_____
    What action needs to be taken to improve the rating?

✔ Summary of comments or concerns:

Name: _____

EXERCISE 5.3: DON'T EXPECT IT TO BE EASY

Type: Reflection — Exploration

Purpose: To provide you with some knowledge and skills so that you can become more culturally competent and identify the best ways to "make it work" for you.

Exercise: In the left column on the following page, identify one or two challenging situations involving diversity issues you have come across during your practicum setting. For each diversity issue, identify the possible effects it may have on your learning needs (middle column). Finally, identify ways in which you might manage those challenges (right column). The effects of differences may be either positive or negative.

Notes on Use

Student: Think of a diversity dilemma or situation you have with a client, your practicum instructor, other staff, or classmate who is of a different racial, cultural, or ethnic background, or gender, sexual orientation, disability, or class. Think of ways to manage and take action on the issue.

Practicum Instructor and *Practicum Tutorial Teacher:* This exercise also works well with a group of students. Provide time for your student (or class) to write down one or two challenging situations or issues of diversity. Give each student the opportunity to share with one another but keep discussion and elaboration to a minimum until all ideas are generated. Record situations on a flip chart.

Select the most interesting, difficult, or challenging dilemmas for the focus of a group discussion. Have your students work in small groups to generate suggestions for discussion and possible resolution. Explore sources and root causes of each dilemma. Look at systemic and structural causes. Ask students what they learned.

• Part Three •

Difference   Effects   Ways to Manage

Name: _____

EXERCISE 5.4: DESIGNER LEARNING

Type: Application

Purpose: To provide you with a guide for your learning needs from educational supervision.

Exercise: As a student, you need to take a very active part in planning, organizing, and directing your learning during supervisory conferences to help maximize the time directed toward your learning. In preparation for your next supervisory conference, the brief outline on the following page can help you plan for it. Fill in the spaces provided before you attend your next conference. Then take the form with you to your meeting.

Notes on Use

Student: Use the planning guide for each supervisory conference by completing an agenda prior to it. By copying this form, you can then have an agenda guide for each week that can serve as notes for each meeting. Provide your practicum instructor with a copy of the agenda *prior* to your meeting. Keep your agendas filed together in your loose-leaf practicum binder.

Practicum Instructor: Go over the student's agenda before you meet.

Practicum Tutorial Teacher: Ask students to complete this exercise for each supervisory conference and keep the agendas in a book as a record of their supervision. Students should hand in to you their record of planning for you to monitor. Also, ask your students to discuss in class the ways they can prepare and plan for their supervision.

SUPERVISION AGENDA AND NOTES   DATED_____

✔ Objectives of next supervisory conference:

✔ Theme, or content, of next supervisory conference:

✔ Detail two situations, issues, or client examples that you need assistance with. Provide your initial impressions or assessment toward problem solving, or an increased understanding of some theme:

✔ Other agenda items:

Name: _____

EXERCISE 5.5: WHAT DO YOU WANT TO KNOW?

Type: Reflection

Purpose: To consider the quality of your educational supervision.

Exercise: From the list of characteristics of educational supervision on the following page, identify those that you think will help maximize your learning needs. Briefly identify contributions that you must make to a positive learning environment. Check the list for contributions your praciticum instructor provides. Reflect on your last educational supervision meeting. How is it going so far?

Notes on Use

Student: Complete the checklist of supervision qualities for things that are important for your learning needs. Think about the last meeting with your practicum instructor in relation to your learning needs. What specific suggestions can you think of to improve the effectiveness of your learning environment?

Practicum Instructor: Discuss with your student what is important in an educational supervision meeting for learning to occur. For example, more discussion on agency policy, role-playing, feedback on written skills, and so forth. Identify which responsibilities are your student's and which are yours.

Practicum Tutorial Teacher: Have students develop a list of ideas about their expectations of educational supervision. Discuss with them (as a group) what they expect from supervision. What does your social work program expect will occur in educational supervision? Are the two perspectives congruent? Discuss ways your students need to take more of a responsibility for their learning needs through educational supervision.

✔ Adequate time is allocated for supervisory conferences:

✔ There are sufficient tasks and workload between conferences:

✔ Communication is clear:

✔ Guidance and consultation takes place:

✔ Overall quality of supervisory process:

✔ Boundaries of the student–practicum instructor relationship are clear:

✔ Feedback occurs:

✔ Teaching takes place:

✔ What I like best about supervision conferences:

✔ What I like least about supervision conferences:

✔ What I can do to improve supervision conferences:

Name: _____

EXERCISE 5.6: HEART AND SOUL

Type: Exploration — Application

Purpose: To provide you with feedback about your developing skills and abilities as a professional social worker. If you are receiving regular feedback from your practicum instructor there will be no surprises about your abilities when it is time for your mid-term and final evaluation.

Exercise: Feedback can be positive and negative. Learning to deal with feedback is difficult. So, how are you doing so far? What is your reaction to or feelings about the feedback you have been receiving from your supervisory conferences, staff, clients, and others? Complete the two items on the following page. Be frank and open.

Notes on Use

Student and *Practicum Instructor:* Discuss the results of the student's analysis. What steps need to be taken to increase the effectiveness of future supervisory conferences?

Practicum Tutorial Teacher: Have your students discuss their experiences of reviewing feedback within their supervisory conferences. Role-play possible student–practicum instructor feedback situations. Discuss these with your students and suggest alternate strategies for feedback improvement.

✔ Write your responses to the *positive* feedback you have received during your supervisory conferences. How are you going to incorporate this feedback into helping you become a professional social worker?

✔ Write your responses to the *negative* feedback you have received during your supervisory conferences. How are you going to incorporate this feedback into helping you become a professional social worker?

Name: _____

EXERCISE 5.7: DIVERSITY DILEMMAS

Type: Reflection — Exploration — Application

Purpose: To provide you with basic knowledge and skills to become a culturally competent social work practitioner.

Exercise: Write responses to the dilemmas on the following two pages in the space provided.

Notes on Use

Student: Respond to the diversity dilemmas as honestly as you can. Discuss with your practicum instructor, other staff, or your classmates. Do you agree or disagree with the way others thought you should have handled the situations? Be prepared to discuss with others.

Practicum Instructor and *Practicum Tutorial Teacher:* Have students complete this exercise in pairs. After discussing their responses with each other, share with the whole group. Have the group decide the best responses. Develop a set of guidelines for social work practice based on the group's collective response.

✔ What would you do if a client refused to see you because of your diversity?

✔ What would you do if you wished to be taken off a case because the client is overtly racist, or sexist, or discriminates in other ways?

✔ What would you do if one of your colleagues in your practicum setting (or elsewhere in the agency) behaved in a manner that was racist, sexist, or discriminatory in other ways?

Chapter Six

*I was uncomfortable in documenting and analyzing
my own work. However, after I sat down with my
practicum instructor, I had concrete things to work with.*

— A Student

The Write Stuff

A GUIDE TO EXAMINING YOUR WORK

E ACH PHASE OF YOUR PRACTICUM experience requires you to examine critically what you do in your practicum setting. This undoubtedly will prepare you for your mid-term and final evaluations. By now, you should have formulated your learning agreement by specifying goals and objectives; you should have discussed your practice objectives and your learning process with your practicum instructor in supervisory conferences; and you should have documented and analyzed your practice activities so that you could review your progress and performance as they pertain to your learning objectives. In short, to this point, a good part of your time has been spent in documenting and writing—all in an effort to meet your individual learning needs.

Documenting your work involves administrative tasks such as putting your client's name, the date of application, and the type of service requested in the client's file. It also involves recording information in certain preplanned ways. This kind of documentation tells you what went on when you provided service and involves your analytical skills. A description of how you handled an individual treatment session and how you analyzed it is an example of using your analytical skills. Documenting and analyzing are important as learning tools and as evidence of what you have accomplished. After all, despite your struggles, you have had your moments of glory, and you would like these to be branded on your practicum instructor's memory as she starts to prepare for your mid-term evaluation (the topic of the next chapter). Examining your work has two initial stages: collecting information, and then making sense of it. All of this takes place in relation to your identified learning goals and objectives.

COLLECTING INFORMATION: OBSERVING AND SCRIPTING

By now you have accumulated various files on different subject areas, all filled with the information you have been collecting. You should have made attempts to collate the information into some coherent pattern—contacts made, tasks accomplished, tasks still to be accomplished, and so forth. Among this vast array, certain records might be particularly important in terms of your mid-term evaluation. These include your journal, notes in your clients' files, notes on supervisory conferences with your practicum instructor, notes from meetings and consultations, and process recordings. Videotapes (and audiotapes as well) also represent an important form of documenting and analyzing what you are doing. In addition, you should have had the opportunity to observe other workers in action. Similarly, this will also give you a chance to document your observations of others.

Documenting Observations of Others

In documenting your observations of others you should utilize a page with two separate columns: one column for a summary of the information acquired from the facts, and a second column for your interpretation of the meaning of that information.

Summary of Information

You may have observed an interview with a client conducted by another staff member. Under the *Summary of Information* heading you can describe what you saw: When and where did the interview take place? Who was present? What use was made of video (or audio) equipment?

What questions were asked? What body language was used? How did the client respond to the interview? Did the interviewer take notes? Were any measuring instruments employed, such as self-administered question-naires? Were specific tasks set for the interviewer or client to complete before the next session? What tasks? What arrangements were made regarding the next session? You need to write all this down in the column on the left side of the page of your documentation.

Interpretation of Information

The right side of the page can then be devoted to your interpretation of each event under an *Interpretation of Information* heading. For example, your observation of an interview between a worker and a couple may have been that the husband was present at the interview. You would then record this under the *Summary of Information* heading. Under your *Interpretation of Information* heading you might remark that this was the first time the husband had attended with his wife. The husband's presence was significant because (1) this interview marked the beginning of couple counseling as opposed to individual counseling, or (2) the husband was becoming more supportive of his wife, or (3) the husband had accom-plished the first major step of acknowledging the existence of a problem and decided to ask for help, or (4) another person, such as a child protective services worker, had indicated to the husband that if he did not attend counseling sessions, worse things might befall him.

If you are not sure which of many possibilities is the correct interpreta-tion, you might make a note to ask the interviewer or your practicum instructor later on, or simply check out your impressions at a later date or interview. Alternately, all might become clear when the husband remarks that he feels he is going "crazy" and has no control of his life, the interviewer is a useless do-gooder, and child protection services has no right to interfere in his business.

In a similar way, you might observe that no video or audio equipment was being used. This was because (1) the equipment was unavailable, (2) this particular interviewer rarely uses such equipment, or (3) the husband voiced a vociferous protest and refused to sign a consent form (which will be discussed subsequently in this chapter). In this connection, you might note later that the interviewer took copious notes because she needed a complete record in order to analyze a difficult interview and because the information was required by another social service agency.

You may think that the interviewer performed well. If so, you can write down in what ways you believe she performed well and share this with her later. If you have questions, your specifically directed praise may motivate her to answer your questions more readily.

You may also feel that the interviewer made some errors and omissions and, had you been the interviewer, you may have taken a different approach. If you have recorded the errors and omissions you believe she may have made, why you feel they were errors, and what you would have done instead, she may be prepared to discuss this with you. Be aware that such discussions are always delicate. The interviewer may perceive your comments not as an attempt to acquire wisdom but as a direct criticism of her abilities. She may be concerned that you will communicate your criticisms to your practicum instructor, who also may be her direct supervisor. She may be afraid that you will discuss the negative aspects of the interview openly with other staff members or even with staff from another agency.

Usually, none of this will occur because your practicum instructor will have selected the staff members you are to observe as carefully as she has selected the clients you are to see. Such workers are normally open to challenge and are ready to consider suggestions, admit to errors, and point out why the errors you noted were not errors at all. Nevertheless, care and sensitivity on your part are also needed.

Documenting the Process: Your Journal

If you try to take accurate, complete, and coherent notes on everything that occurs in the course of a day, you will do little else. Your journal should be a record not of every event but only of significant and meaningful events. For example, you may want to leave out the fact that you had lunch with Pam if all you did was eat and talk about life. On the other hand, if lunch with Pam marked a change in the relationship between the two of you, or if you discussed some vital aspect of a group you both facilitate, this is worthy of note. The difficulty, of course, is deciding what counts as a significant event. Inevitably, you will fail to record a momentous something that did not appear in the least momentous at the time you ignored it.

All you can do is try your best to identify significant events in relation to other events. For example, every learning experience is significant because it relates directly to achieving your learning objectives. Events around relationships are significant because relationships—your own and other people's—affect both your learning and your personal satisfaction in your practicum setting. Supervisory conferences with your practicum instructor are definitely important. So are events that involve contentious issues, because they might be important in the future even if they do not seem so at the time.

Occasionally, despite all of your care, you might become embroiled in a dispute. For example, it might be said that you have unethically shared confidential information with someone else, or you have carried "tales," or you have failed to cooperate with some social worker on a particular project or even by-passed a primary decision maker on a case or project. As you know, you should not discuss one worker's performance with another worker, and you should not discuss your agency at all with members of a different agency. If you have been in the habit of taking notes on what occurred, under what circumstances it occurred, and why you believe it occurred, you will be able to use these notes to defuse the conflict or, in the worst case, to defend your position. Thus it is important for many reasons that your notes be accurate, coherent, and complete.

Another significant documentation area is your reaction to the event you have recorded. Did you feel satisfied after your lunch-time talk with Pam or were you left with a vague feeling that something was wrong? If you took part in a group discussion, did you feel comfortable with the group or did you feel that your suggestions and comments were largely ignored? Did you feel bad about a canceled appointment or an unreturned telephone call? Did you feel good when Mr. Gutman eventually told you his *real* problem?

At the end of the week, when you have written down what events occurred, what they meant, and how you felt about them, you need to write a summary. In other words, you need to pick out the most significant events from your list to see if they form some kind of a pattern. In short, you need to write the "write stuff."

Do not forget that your practicum instructor and liaison may need to read some or all of your journal. Your journal should be reasonably tidy so that it will not embarrass you, and it should be written in a language that will not embarrass you either. For example, you must resist the temptation to express your feelings about some incident or your opinion of a social worker's behavior in the strongest of terms.

Rather than documenting extreme feelings, if you make an attempt to write objectively, taking into account the worker's possible point of view, you might even discover some point of empathy. If this does not occur, a reasoned account of what took place is still more impressive than an outburst of emotion. If you are referring to clients in your journal, it is better to use initials. You will not store your journal with the same careful security as your clients' files and you do not want to risk any accidental breach of confidentiality.

Notes in Clients' Files

Much of your material about clients is recorded in their files. Files tend to be read by people other than the writer, and the information contained in them is not only shared with other social workers but may affect future decisions regarding your client. Take care therefore to write as accurately as possible. If you can justify giving your client the benefit of the doubt, do so. If your comments must be critical or negative, make sure that you have evidence to support your position. Where your comments are not backed up by facts, say they are your impressions or the impressions of others. Do not record impressions as facts. References to other workers must also be made with circumspection since they and others will read what you say.

You might take your material either from a videotape of the interview or from notes you made while it was going on. Such note taking always involves a delicate balance between writing every word verbatim and making a few cryptic scrawls that you hope you can interpret later on. There are also the feelings of your client to be considered. If you write extensively, for example, Mr. Gutman may wonder if something is really wrong with him since you are writing down everything he says. On the other hand, if you write very little, he may think he is not saying anything that is worth writing down.

As always, it is a question of compromise. Write facts—for example, Mr. Gutman's negative relationship with his boss and his gloomy outlook on life, if you are discussing that. Write memory joggers: He mentioned that he was having a great deal of difficulty at work. Write impressions: He is not afraid to go to the union. Particularly, note tasks that you have promised and/or he has promised to accomplish, arrangements for the next session, and any special considerations.

Tell your clients at the beginning of your interviews that you are just going to take a few notes in order to remember important things. If your clients seem uneasy, tell them as you go along what you are writing down. As soon as you can after the interview, amplify your notes and write them in a coherent form. The longer you wait, the more likely it is that you will forget or distort something, particularly if you have seen another client in the meantime.

Notes on Supervisory Conferences

You may have a separate file that you use to prepare for your supervisory conferences. If so, for each reason you should write down the focus, when and where it is to take place, what materials you need to take, what questions you want to ask, and what you hope to have achieved when it is over. In this same file are your notes taken from previous conferences. Record your practicum instructor's analyses and suggestions and write down any tasks that both of you have agreed to perform.

Probably your instructor will also be taking notes, and these notes will guide her when she comes to prepare for your mid-term evaluation. It may be stressful for you to watch her writing if you are not quite sure what she is putting down. Usually, she will be writing what has been said, recording her impressions of the material you have provided, and noting your progress, areas to be worked on, tasks to be accomplished, and so forth. All she is doing is putting her thoughts into written form so that she will not forget about them later. Ideally, everything she writes down should be shared with you.

If you are still uneasy, you might remember that her supervisory notes are usually open to inspection by your practicum liaison. These notes, along with other records, form the basis for your grade (whether pass/fail or letter grade), and your practicum instructor needs documentation to support her impressions and observations of you in the same way that you need documentation to support your impressions of your clients.

Another factor to consider is that some social work programs require students to evaluate their practicum settings at the end of the term. Affiliation with the social work program, via the practicum, is important to your practicum setting, and your instructor wants just as much of a positive evaluation as you do. You therefore have the same responsibility as she does to be frank during your supervisory conferences. The evaluation of your practicum instructor and your setting is the last phase of your field educational experience and is covered in Chapter Nine.

For example, it would not be fair for you to write in your evaluation that you "rarely received relevant feedback" if you had never mentioned the feedback problem to your instructor. In the same way, she would not write, for example, that "Ross's attitude toward support staff is not appropriately professional," unless she had explored with you what she meant by your professional attitude toward support staff and in what ways you fell below her perceived standard. She should provide you with specific examples of your behaviors.

When your supervisory conference session is over, it is a good idea for you to look at your notes in relation to your preparatory material. Did you ask the questions you had intended to ask? If not, why not? If you did, were they answered to your satisfaction? Were you comfortable or uneasy with your practicum instructor's feedback? Was the feedback relevant and sufficient? Were examples given? Did you achieve what you had hoped for during the session? What additional topics were discussed? If you make a brief summary of all this at the end of each session, you may find that patterns begin to emerge.

For instance, you may have felt unhappy with the feedback once or twice because you were going through a difficult period with a difficult client. However, of you *always* feel unhappy with the feedback this may mean that you do not respond well to constructive criticism or that your practicum instructor is unable to make criticisms in a positive, meaningful way.

You can then address this concern with your practicum instructor in your next supervisory conference. If you get useful responses about the feedback, this is definitely a beginning. Getting meaningful feedback is vital to your success as a future social worker. At times, feedback can be threatening. Other times, however, it can be very rewarding. The most important thing for you to remember is to keep saying to yourself that you are a student and you want to learn as much as you can.

RECORDING INFORMATION: VIDEO-RECORDING

Videotaping student-client interviews is an effective method to help you learn practice skills, explore alternative responses, enhance your awareness and sensitivity, improve your understanding and practice effectiveness, and make better use of feedback. Your practicum instructor and liaison expect you to videotape interviews to demonstrate your ability to practice and to reflect upon and learn from your practice.

Guidelines for Taping Interviews

Listed below are a few guidelines that we feel are useful for you to remember when taping interviews with your clients:

✔ Always ask your client for permission to videotape an interview. Be prepared to explain exactly why you want to videotape it, who will see the tape, and what you plan to do with it. It is best to have clients give permission in writing by signing a consent form (see example of taping consent form on the following page).

✔ Present your request in a relaxed manner. If you are uncomfortable with taping, your client may pick up your discomfort. Past experience indicates that clients are usually quite cooperative when they understand that the videotape is a useful tool for enhancing your work with them.

✔ Many persons who have never videotaped interviews before fear that clients will object. In reality, most do not object to being taped. You might explain that you are a student and that taping the interview and going over it afterward with your practicum

TAPING CONSENT FORM
(FOR CLIENT'S FILE)

_____ (name of agency) often finds it helpful to make audio or videotape recordings of sessions between its workers and clients. The tapes are used as valuable tools for education and supervision purposes. They are also helpful when played back to client(s).

_____ (name of agency) recognizes that clients have a right to decide whether or not they wish to have a session taped. The tapes are made only with the client's written consent.

I hereby grant _____ (name of student) permission to make an audio tape _____ or videotape _____ recording of interview(s) held with myself and/or my family provided that such recording will be used solely for educational or therapeutic purposes.

I give my permission for this tape to be seen by (✓ check as desired):

____ the student and the student's supervisor (practicum instructor)
____ other student(s) and staff associated with the agency
____ the student's practicum liaison/practicum tutorial teacher
____ the student's classmates

This tape may be:

• Erased by: _____ (date)

• Kept for educational purpose: Yes _____ No _____

I understand that the need for confidentiality will be explained to the viewer(s) prior to use of this material.

_____
Signature of Client (Date)

_____
Signature of Student (Date)

_____
Signature of Practicum Instructor (Date)

instructor will help you learn and be of better service. It will also give the benefit of the thinking of your instructor and perhaps of other professionals with more experience. Further, if you are able to videotape, you do not need to be concerned with taking written notes and you can devote your full attention to the interview itself. You should advise your clients that the videotapes will be available for them to listen to as well.

✔ Always have the machine clearly visible. Never attempt to hide it or the microphone. Place it in a position that will clearly pick up the client's voice and your own. Avoid placing it near noise sources such as open windows or air conditioners.

Making Taped Recordings

If your interviews are videotaped, there will be no question of your having invented dialogue, as you could do in a process recording. A videotape is obviously preferable to an audiotape because a lot of communication is nonverbal, but the videotape may also be initially more threatening. At first, you may be delighted if the equipment is unavailable, your client refuses to be videotaped, or your practicum instructor fails to mention videotaping as a possibility. However, if you can survive the shock of seeing yourself as you are rather than as you imagine, you will come to rely on the videotape as an important analytical tool.

Your first task is to tell yourself firmly that this has to be done, you will survive it, you will benefit from it, and, more importantly, your increased awareness will benefit your clients. Once you have convinced yourself that all these things are true, your next task is to do it. The two points briefly outlined next may be of some help.

Asking Permission

In most instances, you must have your client's signed consent before you videotape an interview. If you wish that you could forget about the whole matter, your reluctance will readily transfer itself to your client and you will comfortably agree together that it is not a very good idea. You may be even more reluctant with your next client, words will be heard from your practicum instructor, and a useful learning tool will have become an instrument of torture.

It is much more sensible, therefore, to beam affably upon your client, present the taping as a normal part of data-gathering procedures, and assume that the consent form will be signed. It will help your client if you say why you want it. You must remember that you are a student and to provide your client with the best possible service, you may need to be guided by your practicum instructor. The videotapes are to be used by the both of you in an effort to help you better serve your clients.

The Potential Audience

There is also the matter of who is to see it. You will see it, your practicum instructor will see it, your practicum liaison may see it, and your client is more than welcome to see it. However, no one else will view the tape unless you have first obtained explicit written consent from your client. At the end of your practicum, the videotape will be erased unless your practicum instructor wants to keep it as a teaching tool to be used with other social work students. In that case, you will also need to ask for written consent from your client.

By now, your client will probably be quite happy with the idea of being videotaped. You may want to use the tape later to point out to your client, Mr. Gutman, that he really mumbled, shuffled his feet, slouched, and stared at the floor all the time you were role-playing a job interview with him. A few role-plays later, when he has ceased to mumble, stare, and shuffle, you can show him on tape how far he has progressed.

If at the beginning Mr. Gutman is still reluctant to use the videotape, you might suggest a 5- or 10-minute trial run to see how it goes. If it bothers him after those first few minutes, shut it off. If, after all this, Mr. Gutman still refuses written consent, you will just have to try again with your next client.

If you do not want your client to stare at you doubtfully while you fiddle with buttons, give the machine a trial run in some quiet place where you can shout for help if necessary. Once you have learned how it works and practice with it, display it openly in a place where it will pick up you and your client, both visually and audibly. Obviously, you do not want to put the microphone next to the air conditioner or near an open window where the sound of large trucks will drown out most of the recording.

ANALYZING: MAKING SENSE OF INFORMATION

There are two primary methods of analyzing your work. One is using process recordings and the other is using videotaped recordings.

Analyzing Process Recordings

As you will see from your practice methods book, process recordings are written accounts of interviews made after they have taken place. They are useful in addition to audiotapes or videotapes because they can include the interviewer's feelings and interpretations, which may not be the same thing at all as what the client *thinks* took place or what actually *did* take place.

Nevertheless, the process recording is almost as old as social work; it will probably be around for a long time and it has its advantages. For example, if you thought after the interview that you should have said something different to Mr. Gutman, you will be sorely tempted to include the different something in the process recording in place of what you really said. This does nothing to improve accuracy but it does indicate that learning has taken place. The very fact that you were able to analyze critically and improve on your responses says something for process recordings. Since the use of process recordings is to refine your practice skills, and since this book does not deal with skills, you are encouraged to read other books that cover process recordings in depth and offer different ways that they can be organized.

The process recording is a useful teaching-learning tool. It provides you with the opportunity to recall and reflect on any feelings you experienced during your interview. These feelings can then be reviewed and their possible effect on your client can be assessed. By providing an approximate text of the interview, the process recording allows your practicum instructor and liaison to follow your interview, see the steps you have taken, and provide you with useful feedback.

Through a process recording, you can sort out the facts from your feelings and your hypotheses or speculations about the client's thoughts and feelings. You can reflect upon the *process* as well as the *content* of the interview. You can consider what you *know* along with what you *sense* about the client and her situation. Your reflections are an important source of data about your work, your effectiveness, your intervention choices, and your practice decisions. A process recording is a valuable tool for structuring these reflections.

Your practicum instructor or liaison may see problems or strengths that you may not have picked up on, and thereby alert you and help guide your professional development. This important learning experience invites you to gain knowledge about yourself and how you relate to other people. Space is reserved in the process recording format for you to identify feelings relating to the interactions you have had with your clients. Your practicum instructor and liaison can then assist you in understanding your feelings and behaviors in reference to you interactions with your clients.

When doing process recordings you should remember two important points: names and identifying details in the recording should be altered to preserve confidentiality, and the process recording should be done as soon as possible after the interview so that it will be as accurate and complete as possible.

Analyzing Taped Recordings

An interesting exercise is to critique your interview before you view the tape. You will learn from this how closely your memory parallels reality, and subsequently you may be more effective when you have to analyze an interview without a videotape.

When you view the tape, look for themes. Do you constantly allow your client to wander off the topic? Do you regularly have difficulty in persuading Mr. Gutman to express specific cognitions rather than vague and rambling feelings? Do you express feelings yourself or are you uncomfortable telling a client that you are uncomfortable? Do you hasten to fill in every conversational gap? Do you unconsciously pick at your teeth, play with your hair, shuffle your feet, or overuse your hands in gesturing?

If you watch the tape first without your practicum instructor, you will be able to select which parts to show her in case she does not have time to watch it all. These parts should obviously relate to any problems you are having with either of your interviewing techniques or with your client, but you need not restrict yourself to problems.

If you did something well, particularly if it was something you did badly before, show her that part too. She needs to know your strengths as well as your weaknesses. When analyzing your videotape, look at the whole interview as well at selected segments of it. Identify parts of the interview that you think are positive representations of your work and learning. These also need to be included in your mid-term and final evaluations.

Analyzing the Whole Interview

In analyzing the interview as a whole:

✔ Identify the purpose of the interview. You should be directed toward formulating a statement of purpose that is concise, clear, and specific in relation to the proposed interview. The statement of purpose should show the relatedness between this interview and any previous work and should also reflect your awareness of the particular function of your practicum setting and of your client's capacity and motivation.

✔ Describe the interview. You should record your general impressions of the physical and emotional climate at the outset of the interview and, more specifically, its impact on your client. Significant changes in the client's appearance and surroundings are also important.

✔ Present the content of the interview. This part of the record should be devoted to the actual description of the interaction during the interview. However, rather than a verbatim account this should be a selective review of the salient issues, themes, and topics. The length of this section of your recording depends on your stage of development and learning patterns. It should:

• Include a description of how the interview began.

• Contain pertinent factual information.

• Include a discussion of the process of the interview, how it unfolded, and the influences on the part both you and your client had on impacting the outcome.

• Provide a description of how the interview ended.

• Link theory and knowledge to practice. You should identify the source of experience you drew upon to inform the decisions that were taken during the interview. This process gradually develops into conceptual thinking as you begin to integrate course content and theoretical material with your practice skills in an actual interview.

• Reflect on practice. You should reflect on the content and process of your interview in relation to its purpose and final outcome. This includes identifying your strengths and weaknesses in the interview and some directions for your future work.

Analyzing a Selected Segment

In analyzing a selected segment of an interview we recommend a six-column format. There are other formats that you can follow, and it may be advisable for you to ask your practicum instructor which specific format she would like you to use.

- Column I: Verbatim account. This should be a transcribed record (or as close to total recall) of what was said in the interview. It should include both your statements and those of your client.

- Column II: Your feelings. This column allows you to identify what you were feeling at the time the verbal exchange was taking place. This column is for you to link your feelings with your actions.

- Column III: Communication skill. This column allows you to label or identify the specific communication skill(s) you are using.

- Column IV: Phase. This column identifies the phase of the interview, such as, engaging, contracting, middle phase, work phase, or termination phase.

- Column V: Alternatives statements. The column provides a space where you can propose an alternative response. If you had it to do over again what might you have preferred to say? This column will improve your future performance with clients. It is always useful for you to know what you would have done differently.

- Column VI: Practicum instructor's comments. This column provides an opportunity for your practicum instructor to make notes and provide feedback to you. You should leave plenty of room in this column as practicum instructors usually comment at length if space is available.

SUMMARY

Documenting your activities is an important learning tool and it evidences what you have accomplished. By the time you reach your mid-term evaluation, you will have accumulated a number of records, including your journal, notes in your clients' files, notes on your supervisory conferences that you had with your practicum instructor, and your process recordings—in addition to your audiotapes and videotapes.

Your journal should be a record of your learning experience. Much of it will be narrative description, but you may want to record some items under two distinct headings: information obtained and interpretation of the information. This two-column format is very useful when you have observed an interview conducted by another social worker or when you are trying to integrate new information with material you already know and are familiar with.

Your journal should contain not every event that occurs during your practicum but only significant events. Often it is difficult to decide what counts as a significant event, however. Essentially, assume that all learning experiences count, including your supervisory conferences with your practicum instructor and all events concerned with relationships or contentious issues. Your journal should never use client names because of confidentiality considerations.

Notes made in your clients' files should be as accurate and objective as possible, because such notes can affect future decisions made regarding your client. The material in your clients' files is derived in part from interviews, so it is also important that you keep accurate records of what occurred during your interviews. Note taking during client interviews is a delicate matter. You will probably need to write something, but the act of writing will also distract you from giving your concentrated attention to your client. If you plan to write up your interview as soon as possible after it has finished, you will be required to write less while it is actually in progress.

Your notes on supervisory conferences with your practicum instructor will help you to determine the effectiveness of these sessions. You will know to what degree you have achieved your learning objectives set for the session and you may be able to perceive patterns of communication or reaction running through the sessions. When you evaluate your practicum instructor and setting (Chapter Nine), you will have documented evidence on which to base your evaluations.

Process recordings are written accounts of interviews made after the interviews have taken place. They are less accurate and objective than videotapes, but they may enable you to analyze critically your own responses to your client and substitute more appropriate responses, as well as to formulate assessments of your client. You will not have time to write a process recording after every interview, but you should write some at the beginning, middle, and end of your practicum. You can also use this type of recording as a learning tool if you have a difficult client or feel a lack of progress.

A videotape will provide you with an accurate and objective record of your interview, but you may also find it somewhat intimidating. Because it is such an invaluable way of providing feedback, you will have to overcome your initial fears and reduce the same fears in your client. Your client's written consent is necessary, and it is important that you are clear about what the tape is for, who will have access to it, and what will happen to it once your practicum is over.

Your strengths will be revealed through your documentation; remember, too, that the ability to document activities completely, coherently, and accurately is also a strength.

Name: _____

EXERCISE 6.1: THE INTERVIEW REVIEW

Type: Reflection

Purpose: To reflect upon the content and process of an interview.

Exercise: Using a recent interview, answer the questions on the following three pages.

Notes on Use

Student: Complete the interview review. Then discuss it with your practicum instructor.

Practicum Instructor: Provide your student with feedback on the quality of the interview review.

Practicum Tutorial Teacher: Have students role-play with other students using findings from the analyses of their interview reviews. One student should assume the client role. Discuss giving feedback in the debriefing time.

THE INTERVIEW REVIEW

Student's name: _____

Date: _____

Client's initials: _____

✔ Objectives for this interview:

✔ Content themes of what you and your interviewee talked about:

✔ Analyze the interviewee's behavior in relation to affect, emotional tone, body language, and speech patterns:

✔ Describe a sample interaction:

✔ Do you think you and your interviewee had the same expectations for the interview? If not, discuss any differences:

✔ Identify what was accomplished in your interview:

✔ Identify what increased your understanding of your interviewee situation:

✔ What are your next steps? Include collaborative work (if indicated):

✔ What did you like and dislike about the interview?

✔ What would you do differently? Why?

✔ What would you do the same? Why?

✔ What would you like to discuss at the next interview? Why?

Name: _____

EXERCISE 6.2: PROCESS RECORDING

Type: Application — Reflection — Explanation

Purpose: To consider how completing process recordings contributes to your understanding of social work practice.

Exercise: Complete a process recording using a format given to you by your practicum instructor.

Notes on Use

Student: Decide with your practicum instructor which client interview you should do and which process recording format you should use. Hand your process recording in to your practicum instructor for her comments. Discuss in detail.

Practicum Instructor: Comment on the quality of your student's process recording, including his or her ability to interpret interview content and the client's nonverbal behavior. Examine and discuss your student's appropriate "use of self."

Practicum Tutorial Teacher: Have your students share the learning they derived from their process recordings. Review the different ways of documenting process. Have your students examine which types of documentation are facilitating their learning goals and objectives.

BASIC INFORMATION FOR YOUR PROCESS RECORDING:

✔ Background information:

✔ Statement of purpose and goals for the interview:

✔ How did you prepare for the interview:

✔ Describe the interaction in each of the phases of the interview in a narrative style: beginning, middle, and end:

✔ Reflect on your skills, your reactions, and your thoughts and feelings in each phase:

✔ Leave space for your practicum instructor to comment:

Name: _____

EXERCISE 6.3: THE VIDEO RECORDER

Type: Reflection — Application

Purpose: To gain a beginning comfort with taping your work, as well as the use of role-play to enhance your learning needs.

Exercise: Ask another student to pretend that he or she is a client from your practicum setting and role-play 10 minutes of a beginning interview with your classmate. Videotape your session. Remember to start your interview by first getting permission to tape it. Take brief notes of your role-play interview on the following page.

Notes on Use

Student: Review the videotape for technical quality as well as your impression of your beginning interviewing skills. Discuss in detail.

Practicum Instructor: Watch the tape and give your student feedback on the interviewing skills used.

Practicum Tutorial Teacher: List the beginning interviewing skills that your student used and discuss in detail.

• Part Three •

INTERVIEW NOTES:

Name: _____

EXERCISE 6.4: WRITING STORIES

Type: Exploration

Purpose: To explore and understand sensitive cultural issues that have a personal meaning.

Exercise: Write a brief story on the following page about your experience of an ingrained racial or cultural attitude, prejudice, or stereotype. You may have been the oppressor or the oppressed. What meaning does the story hold for you? How does it relate to your practicum experience?

Notes on Use

Student: Share your story with someone else. Does the telling of the story reveal any new meaning to you? How can you make use of this understanding in your practicum setting?

Practicum Instructor and *Practicum Tutorial Teacher:* Ask your students to consider how their racial attitudes, prejudices, and stereotypes might affect their learning and their work in the practicum setting.

• Part Three •

YOUR BRIEF STORY:

Name: _____

EXERCISE 6.5: CULTURAL GENOGRAMS

Type: Reflection — Application

Purpose: To reflect on the impact of cultural issues on family interactions and develop skill in using genograms.

Exercise: Draw a cultural genogram (on a separate piece of paper) of your own family of origin. Identify the attitudes and beliefs regarding those who are "different" from you. Identify some of the messages that you have received over the years about families and "outsiders" that are culturally derived.

Notes on Use

Student: Draw an intergenerational genogram and label the beliefs and attitudes.

Practicum Instructor: Ask your students what they learned from doing their cultural genograms. How does this type of learning relate to their practicum settings?

Practicum Tutorial Teacher: Ask your students to discuss ways they can address the issues they identified from their cultural genograms.

Chapter Seven

How Is It Going So Far?

B Y NOW YOU HAVE REACHED a point where it is time to find out how well you are doing in your practicum. You have been involved in a process of building up your knowledge base, through trial and error, through your various experiences, and through analyzing many of your behaviors. You are preparing diligently, performing zealously, and recording industriously. The time has come. You want to know how well you are doing it! The date and the hour have been set. Your practicum instructor awaits. It is time for your evaluation. You have had the luxury of time to be reflective and analytical of your experiences.

PEOPLE AFFECTED BY EVALUATIONS

Evaluation plays a key role in your development as a professional social worker. Evaluation helps you to minimize future failures and maximize your future strengths. With evaluation, you should discover "what works" for you, which will help you to be in a position to develop "your own model of practice." Evaluations should be useful to you, the profession, your practicum instructor, and your social work program. Let us now turn to how evaluations are useful for the profession.

Evaluation as It Affects the Profession

During an observation of an interview with a couple, you may have heard the husband remark that the interviewer was a useless do-gooder. In a few cases, in fact, he may have been correct. A few social workers *are* not doing "it" very well. Some proud individuals, who hold BSWs and MSWs, have no idea about why they do the things they do. In some cases, this is not their fault. They were not taught what to do and they were not corrected when they failed to do it. They moved passively through their practicums, obtaining "satisfactory" after "satisfactory," *relating* well to all the world, but *learning* minimal amounts in relation to concrete helping skills. They were then released to impart their nonlearning upon trusting clients, frustrated employers, doubting members of other professions, and innocent beginning social work students.

From an ethical point of view, it is the trusting clients and innocent students who suffer the most. After all, a frustrated employer can always resort to termination. From the point of view of the social work profession, however, it is the doubt implanted in other professional disciplines that is most problematic.

Tradespeople building a house assume that the carpenters, plumbers, electricians, and others will each do their respective jobs. A plumber who cannot plumb is not regarded with favor by the general contractor and the rest of the building team. If a number of plumbers appear to be unable to plumb, the whole of the plumbing trade falls into disrepute. In the same way, a multidisciplinary team of professionals caring for a mutual client do not look with favor on an inadequate social worker. And numbers of inadequate social workers result in a general disrespect for the social work profession. A low-status profession tends to attract low-status students who become, in their turn, low-status workers and practicum instructors. And so the mess continues.

There are a number of ways out of this dilemma, however. First, the present coterie of inadequate social workers could be identified and fired. This is impractical. Second, incoming students could be subjected to a more stringent selection process in an attempt to improve the general standard. There are advocates for this approach. Third, the drift of an inadequate student from "satisfactory" to "satisfactory" to "graduation" could be stopped at the first "satisfactory." There are advocates for this approach too, but there are a number of barriers impeding its implementation. These barriers have to do with the component of social work that is defined as "art," and the various reactions of the student, the program, and the practicum instructor to an unsatisfactory practicum rating. For now, let us think for a moment about the feelings of your practicum instructor.

Evaluation as It Affects
Your Practicum Instructor

A practicum instructor acts as one of the gatekeepers for the social work profession. She may have seen many students and many professional social workers. She knows, first hand, that incompetent social work practice can injure clients, produce negative feelings about the agency in the community, and have a damaging impact on other professionals. She also knows that most students admitted to your social work program have sufficient academic ability to pass their courses and that most do pass. It is in the practicum setting that learning is turned into practice.

It is in the practicum where students become competent social workers. This is the place where good students can be most easily differentiated from poor ones. Generally, this responsibility falls upon the practicum instructor to make the differentiation. If she does not perform this task objectively and conscientiously, she is failing in her duty to our clients, our community, and our profession.

On the other hand, your practicum instructor understands the impact of a negative evaluation upon you. She has taught you. She has formed a relationship with you. She may personally like you very much. As a social worker, she is trained to be nonjudgmental. She spends her working life trying to be helpful, trying to be positive, giving the benefit of the doubt whenever possible, and being very careful to accept people for what they are and to avoid imposing her own values on them.

Yet now she is in a position where she is required to make a judgment. She is required to impose professional standards and values—upon you—and may have to write that, in her opinion, you have failed to meet these standards. It is not surprising that many practicum instructors hesitate before doing this. They agonize over the decision. They defend the student in their own minds by telling themselves that it might have been different with another practicum instructor in another practicum setting. Then they think about the student's future clients who will inevitably be hurt if a poor student is allowed to continue.

There is also the matter of the practicum instructor's responsibility as a teacher. Teachers of adults are responsible only for teaching; they are not responsible for ensuring that students learn. Nevertheless, if the student fails to learn, there is always a nagging doubt in the practicum instructor's mind: Perhaps the material could have been presented differently. Perhaps there could have been more or different feedback, a different client, a different project.

Even when the practicum instructor knows she has done all she could for the student, there is still a lingering temptation to blame herself anyway, to let the student pass the first practicum in the hope that the next one will bring improvement. Fortunately, there is the consultation process with the practicum liaison to assist both you and your practicum instructor in the process of evaluation.

Evaluation as It Affects Your Program

The emphasis on the evaluation of learning will differ in each social work program. Some programs require a formal mid-term evaluation of your progress during your practicum while others do not. Some programs formally evaluate their practicum instructors while others do not. In addition, some programs formally evaluate each practicum setting. Then there are programs that do not view evaluation quite this formally. Above all, the evaluation of learning assists in providing a continuing quality practicum not only for you but for clients as well.

To complicate matters further, a negative evaluation can cause friction with your social work program. Most of the time the practicum instructor only recommends the grade; it is the program, via the practicum liaison, that assigns it and makes it official. Therefore, the practicum instructor must have the full support of your social work program if the evaluation is to have a real effect. In general, administrators of social work programs like to know that they turn out competent social work students. They may be tempted to blame the practicum instructor for the failure, particularly if the student is academically bright, has an engaging personality, or has otherwise won favor with the social work faculty.

If the standards of the classroom courses are lower than those of the practicum, the practicum liaison may not agree that the student should be given an unsatisfactory mid-term evaluation. She may transfer the student to another practicum setting or bring pressure to bear on the practicum instructor to change her mind, perhaps through the practicum instructor's own supervisor or someone more senior in the agency's hierarchical structure. However, this is unusual.

Rarely will a social work program not support the recommendation of a practicum instructor, especially if she can document her own teaching methods, the learning opportunities afforded to the student, and the student's performance in specific learning objectives.

Evaluation as It Affects You

Obviously, the person most affected by the evaluation is you. If there has been good communication between you and your practicum instructor, the mid-term evaluation should hold no surprises. Nevertheless, there is a difference between being told that some area needs improvement and seeing a written comment such as, "Jim seems disorganized with regard to administrative matters and fails to meet deadlines."

What about those time sheets you failed to turn in? Your practicum instructor has explained the importance of time sheets on many occasions, far too often in fact. But to you they remain a nagging chore. You feel vaguely guilty about them and vaguely defiant. After all, you did the important client-related work. But, above all, you had hoped that they would not be mentioned.

Now that they have been mentioned, what does this mean in terms of your overall evaluation? The answer, of course, depends on a number of factors. First, how often were you late presenting your time sheets? Once, twice, or on a regular basis? Second, is the problem only time sheets or do the time sheets reflect a general, disrespectful attitude toward administrative duties? Perhaps you feel that writing reports, submitting statistics, and doing paperwork is a silly waste of time and you are not about to perform a task that you feel is a waste of time. Perhaps you have said so, or you think you have made your opinion clear by staring at the floor whenever your practicum instructor mentions time sheets.

One of the learning goals set by some social work programs is that students must be able to *"function effectively within an organizational context."* This can mean a number of things. As we pointed out in Chapter Four, you were advised to look at your practicum evaluation form and derive your learning goals in part from your program's required minimum standards. For example, you may have set out four objectives that more precisely define functioning in an organizational context. Remember that objectives are more specific than goals.

Objective 1 may have stated that you should have *"demonstrated the ability to work within and interpret [your] practicum setting's policies, structures, and functions to clientele and others."* Working within agency policies means that essential paperwork should be submitted when required. Similarly, Objective 2 may have stated that you should have *"demonstrated the ability to describe and analyze the relationship between agency policies and service delivery."* This means, in part, that you should understand *why* you have to do paperwork.

For example, an accumulation of time sheets might have provided long-term, documented evidence that staff members spend an average of 30 percent of their time on administrative duties and that this average has increased by 10 percent in the last five years. In other words, they are now spending 10 percent less time than they did five years ago on other duties, such as service to clients. Eventually, the agency's board of directors may address this problem by reducing the paperwork, hiring another secretary, updating the computer system, or reallocating responsibility for paperwork. But these decisions can only be made on the basis of documented evidence.

Failing to submit your time sheet before the deadline means that you have not met Objective 1. Staring sullenly at the floor when time sheets are mentioned means that you have not met Objective 2. All is not yet lost, however. There are two other objectives that you may have met perfectly. For example, you may have helped Ms. Valoroso obtain subsidized day care for her son Leon; thus, you have "*demonstrated [your] ability to identify and link available services, resources, and opportunities to meet the needs of the client system,*" your third objective.

You may have written a brilliant report in which you linked a growing number of single, working parents in the community to inadequate day care facilities and to an increasing number of cases of child neglect. This report "*demonstrated [your] ability to understand the broad social issues facing the organization and the community*" (Objective 4). In addition, you may have tactfully and sympathetically explained to Ms. Valoroso that agency policy requires you to make a home visit and you cannot complete the necessary forms if she is out every time you call. This masterly interpretation of agency policy to a client refers to Objective 1 and may balance out your lack of performance with the time sheets.

The whole evaluation is a matter of balance. Your practicum instructor will note areas for improvement with regard to organizational functioning: time sheets and sullen staring. She will also note your accomplishments: the brilliant report, the provision of subsidized day care, and the tactful explanation to Ms. Valoroso.

Social work programs differ in the way they define the various areas of functioning, in the way they assess them, and in the way they evaluate their social work students and practicum as a whole. Your program's evaluation form is more than likely different in some way from the one we present in Appendix B. The learning objectives may be assessed on a 1 to 5 scale, a 1 to 10 scale, as poor/satisfactory/excellent, or in some other way. The practicum as a whole may be rated on a point scale, on a pass/fail basis, or on a credit/no credit basis.

The only flaw in the evaluation system, as we have previously indicated, is that *subjectivity* is necessarily present in the whole affair. Your practicum instructor will have records, written and taped, to support her opinion of your performance in various areas, but nevertheless it is an opinion. Some practicum instructors' standards are higher than others; some practicum settings' requirements are more stringent than others. The same student turning in the same performance may be assessed as satisfactory in one practicum setting and outstanding in another, or as poor and outstanding, respectively, by different practicum instructors in the same practicum setting.

You may think that this is not fair. In fact, you are quite right, but the unfairness is largely unavoidable given the present state of the profession. No agreement has been reached among social workers as to precisely what having a BSW or MSW degree means; that is, the body of knowledge that students must possess upon graduation is not clearly defined. And because the body of knowledge has not been defined, the phases on the road to acquiring it cannot be defined either.

The result is that the learning goals and objectives demanded of a social work student in the practicum are decided independently by the various social work programs and are recorded in a way that is both inexact and open to various interpretations. Anything that is open to interpretation will inevitably be interpreted differently by different practicum instructors according to their own standards of social work. Your mid-term and final evaluations are thus inherently subjective. This will remain so until our profession has developed standardized criteria by which social work students can be assessed. Practically, the profession's delineation of standardized criteria probably will not happen while you are in your practicum, so it may be a good idea to go with what your program currently uses.

The subjectivity will work in one of two ways: either you will receive a lower assessment than you might in a different situation or you will receive a higher assessment. If you receive a higher assessment rating, you will naturally be delighted, but the delight may be short-lived. In your next practicum, where the standards may be higher, the level of performance considered as "outstanding" in your previous practicum now may be considered "weak." You may complain that *this* practicum instructor is unfair; whereas, you really experienced the unfairness in the prior practicum, which failed to prepare you properly for the second one. In the event that both practicum instructors have the same low standards, your delight may last until you perform poorly in your first job or until your inadequate training allows you to injure your first unfortunate client.

If you receive a low assessment rating, you may be indignant. You may compare your assessment with that of another student who, in your opinion, did not work harder or achieve more than you yet he received an "excellent" rating and you received "satisfactory." There are two things to remember here.

First, you are not in a position to *know* what learning assignments the other student had. You may think you know but you have not examined his work with the same attention or from the same knowledge base as has his practicum instructor.

Second, you do not know what difficulties he had to contend with.

Perhaps he dealt nonjudgmentally and effectively with an abusive, alcoholic mother when his own mother was also abusive and alcoholic.

The question of making allowances for the skills and backgrounds of different students is always a difficult one for the practicum instructor. A practicum assessment is supposed to reflect the actual level of skills attained, not the number of problems the student solved in order to get there. Nevertheless, the problem-solving process in itself says something about the student. A student who has had to overcome her own prejudices to attain a certain skill level has learned more than one who has not; moreover, she has demonstrated self-awareness, self-control, and an ability to use herself for the client's benefit.

All other things being equal, a student who has struggled to achieve will probably be given a slightly higher assessment rating than another student who has reached the same skill level without a struggle. If this does not seem fair, remember that most practicum instructors look for two things: evidence that learning has taken place and evidence that the student has the ability to learn.

You may resent your "satisfactory" rating because you have never before been *only* a "satisfactory" student. You have always been an "outstanding" student, a joy to your practicum instructor and a source of assistance to other, less talented peers. The first obvious point here is that a student who is outstanding in the classroom is not necessarily outstanding in the field; similarly, a social work instructor who is an "expert" in a particular subject may not teach it very well. The second point is that "satisfactory" is not to be despised. "Satisfactory" means "*completely satisfactory.*" It means that you have reached the required basic learning objectives and you are fully competent as a social worker at your level of training. If you never saw a client until two months ago, if you never worked in the field before or never worked at all before, attaining a "satisfactory" rating is no easy accomplishment. It should be a source of pride.

When all this is said, you may still be unhappy. If you can manage it, discuss your unhappiness with your practicum instructor during the mid-term evaluation conference.

THE EVALUATION CONFERENCE

An evaluation conference, like your supervisory conferences, will be far more productive if you have prepared for it. You should have the same evaluation form that your practicum instructor has for both the mid-term and final evaluation. You know what areas you are to be evaluated on and what evidence is to be used to indicate if you have reached your learning objectives. You can therefore evaluate yourself. For example, in what ways have you demonstrated that you can function effectively in a professional context (Goal 1), in an organizational context (Goal 2), in knowledge-directed practice (Goal 3), and within an evaluative context (Goal 4)? In what ways have you failed to demonstrate these capacities? What overall assessment rating would you give yourself and, more importantly, why?

Next, to what degree have you achieved your learning objectives? To what degree have you not achieved them? How were your learning goals related to your program's and your practicum setting's required standards? How were your assignments related to your objectives? Which assignments did you do well and which did you need to practice more? What does this information tell you about what you still need to achieve? How can you revise your learning goals and objectives to reflect your progress to date and the progress yet to be made?

If you have processed all these criteria ahead of time and written down your reasons for rating yourself the way you did, you will be better prepared to assimilate the feedback given to you during the evaluation conference. You will also be in a position to ensure that all of your triumphs have been taken into account.

In the meeting itself, it may be made clearer to you as never before that your practicum instructor *is* the instructor and you are the student. This obvious power imbalance may be intensified if your practicum liaison is also present at the meeting. Now there are two of them, who you may feel are positioned at the other end of the room in hawk-eyed, silent judgment.

The first thing to remember is that the hawk-eyed judgment is an illusion, mainly brought about by your own level of stress. The primary purpose of an evaluation, particularly your mid-term evaluation, is to evaluate your growth to date and to facilitate your growth for the next half of your practicum experience. The idea behind all of this is for you to summarize your achievements for the benefit of your practicum setting, your social work program, and yourself so that you can all see clearly what remains to be achieved.

This summary of achievements is brought about by conversation with your practicum instructor. Now is your chance to register a concern if there is anything on the evaluation form that does not seem fair. You might, for example, bring to your instructor's attention a particularly brilliant interview which you do not think she took fully into account. Or you might mention that you have submitted your time sheets before the deadline on the last three occasions, thus demonstrating a capacity "*to function in an organizational context*" and a desire to improve.

Your concern must be reasoned, focused, and based on documented evidence and examples. Your instructor's response will then also be reasoned, focused, and based on documented evidence and examples. She may explain to you that your brilliant interview was balanced, in her opinion, by a series of other, not-so-brilliant interviews with examples and explanations provided in the practicum evaluation form. She may tell you that although you have improved in the matter of time sheets, you did not submit this or that report, or perhaps a statistical analysis.

You can respond to these critical appraisals in a number of ways. The easiest and least productive is to become defensive and angry, or defensive and silent, or just defensive. It may be hard for you to hear your work criticized, particularly in the presence of your practicum liaison and most particularly if you interpret the comments as a criticism of yourself. If you can avoid becoming defensive about the negatives, you might be able to hang on to the positives, and there will be positives. Your instructor will know how to use your positive qualities to provide a balanced appraisal of your competencies.

If you can accept the positives and negatives as equally merited, you may then be able to approach the real purpose of the evaluation: to guide your future growth by revising your learning contract in the light of your present achievements. Some of the learning objectives you wrote down at the beginning of your practicum may now seem almost trivial. For example, you may have written as one of your learning objectives that you wanted to learn *"how to engage clients."*

As it turns out, by now, engaging clients is almost second nature; your problem is to stop them from deluging you with their life histories and to keep them focused on the issue at hand. You may agree with your practicum instructor that the engagement objective has been achieved. Your objective instead, if this is only the mid-term evaluation, may be *"to learn to clarify purpose with clients and attend to the emotional content of individuals, or deal with conflict."*

Some learning objectives may seem irrelevant or unattainable; others, obvious now in the light of experience, should have been omitted entirely. Your task, immediately after the mid-term evaluation, will be to revise your learning contract, indicating which objectives need to be pared down or supplemented, which have been achieved, and which have been newly formulated based on identified deficiencies. As before, you will need to discuss these learning objectives with your practicum instructor and get the revised contract approved, in writing, by both your practicum instructor and liaison.

AN UNSATISFACTORY RATING

Even if you suffered some disappointment during your mid-term evaluation, the disappointment will soon pass. One exception is when an "unsatisfactory" assessment threatens your passing the practicum which, in turn, will threaten your social work career.

It is extremely rare that a student is rated "unsatisfactory" without a preliminary warning and a great deal of preliminary work on the part of the practicum instructor. In other words, you will not walk into the mid-term evaluation conference expecting a "satisfactory" and walk out having ignominiously "failed." An "unsatisfactory" should follow only from an identified and fairly major problem that has persisted despite efforts of your practicum instructor, your practicum liaison, and you to solve it. Such problems usually fall into one of the two categories that follow.

Attitude Toward Learning

Becoming defensive in the face of a disappointing evaluation is not productive or desirable, but it is perhaps excusable. However, if you are *habitually* defensive, if you *always* respond to criticism with denial or anger, it will be impossible for your practicum instructor to teach you. If she cannot teach you, it will be impossible for you to achieve your minimum learning goals and objectives that are required for you to pass your practicum.

Your practicum instructor will always make allowances for a family crisis, an ailing automobile, or a life-threatening illness that keeps you away from the agency for a day or two. If the illness is really life-threatening, or if you have really suffered some personal disaster, arrangements may be made for you to make up the lost time, extend the practicum over a longer period of time, or even withdraw from the practicum with an "incomplete." An "incomplete" means that you can finish the practicum at a later date after you have coped with your personal disaster.

If you habitually avoid certain situations, clients, or types of client problems and issues, offering flimsy excuses, if you are frequently late, or if you take two-hour lunch breaks or go home early, your practicum instructor will mention it to you. If you fail to mend your ways after repeated reminders, the result may very well be an "unsatisfactory" rating at your mid-term evaluation.

Suitability to Social Work

Not all people are cut out to be social workers. Some are naturally judgmental or abrupt in manner; some are overly businesslike or unapproachable; some are reserved to the point of coldness; some expect perfection from themselves and others. These kinds of personal characteristics are difficult to overcome and have a negative effect on relationships with clients. They are also problematic for the practicum instructor who has to advise her student to look for another career.

She may point out gently to you that none of your clients have ever come back. She may point out, again gently, why she thinks this has occurred. She may try to help you develop different ways of relating to people. Eventually, however, she will have to tell you that a different career might be more suitable and, if you will not voluntarily withdraw, she will have to recommend a failing grade to your practicum liaison.

Also, some of the most conscientious social work students are not ready for professional practice. If it seems to your practicum instructor that you have not yet developed the readiness required to be a social worker, she may advise you to withdraw for a year or two, gain some life experience, and then come back. Such advice is rarely well received because a student who needs to hear it will probably reject it. The only answer then for the practicum instructor is to assess the student as "unsatisfactory" and to document the reasons in writing to the practicum liaison.

Similarly, the student who has an emotional problem or a crisis going on in her life presents a particularly difficult dilemma for the instructor. Very rarely will a student in a practicum setting exhibit bizarre behavior or some other evidence of emotional upset. The practicum instructor, who is a trained and experienced social worker as well as a practicum instructor, cannot help but be aware that the student needs professional assistance. Normally, she will reach this conclusion long before the mid-term evaluation and will advise the student to obtain counseling outside the practicum setting. You cannot help others until you have your own life in order.

Unprofessional behavior usually involves some breach of the *Code of Ethics* (see Appendix A), not out of ignorance but because the student does not seem to think the *Code* is important. For example, discussing the confidential affairs of clients in a loud voice in the local coffee shop may well earn you an "unsatisfactory." So may habitual failure to lock up client files, sending confidential file material by fax, spreading client or agency tales with intent to harm, or other behaviors that demonstrate little regard for the client or the agency.

YOUR REACTIONS

If you are really unhappy with the results of the evaluation, the first obvious step is to discuss it with your practicum instructor and liaison. This process may possibly result in some form of a compromise. For example, you may agree to withdraw from the practicum rather than receive an "unsatisfactory." You then may have an opportunity to try a new practicum again at a later date in another setting, but your practicum instructor, your practicum liaison, and your social work program must all agree that you be allowed to withdraw.

If the "unsatisfactory" has not resulted from a major problem but is more an accumulation of smaller things, your practicum instructor may allow you to finish the practicum, provided that you show a definite improvement in your activities in relation to specific learning objectives.

For a limited period, if she still hopes the problem can be resolved, your practicum instructor may even assume a more supportive role during your supervisory conferences. Supervisory conferences are not therapy sessions. You are not a client, and your personal problems are your own business unless they are interfering with your work. If they are interfering, your practicum instructor may probe delicately in an effort to help you perform at a satisfactory level. As much as your practicum instructor might personally like to help you, though, the goal of her probing will be to increase your practicum performance; it is not the traditional goal of therapy. She may need to refer you for personal counseling.

If you cannot agree with your practicum instructor and liaison to withdraw, seek counseling, accept a probationary practicum, or whatever is deemed appropriate, you may decide to appeal your practicum instructor's recommendation. The first step in this process is to determine your social work program's appeal procedures concerning mid-term grades. You may also consult your faculty advisor if one is assigned to you, or your practicum director.

If their decision is that the assessment was justified and you are still unhappy, your only recourse is a formal university appeal. Appeal procedures vary considerably from one university to another and you should investigate the procedure at your university very carefully before you begin. We strongly urge you to think twice about appealing a failing grade in your practicum. It has been our experience that practicum instructors and liaisons are very accurate in their judgments in reference to "weeding out" unsuitable social work students.

If it is the opinion of your practicum instructor, your practicum liaison, your faculty advisor, and the practicum director that you should fail at mid-term, we suggest that you spare future clients the effects of your inadequate practice skills by withdrawing from the social work program altogether. Students rarely appeal mid-term evaluations. Finally, it is likely that your evaluation will pass without trauma and will fulfill its function of assessing and redirecting your growth.

SUMMARY

Your evaluation affects not only you but also your practicum instructor and your social work program. Your practicum instructor acts as one of the gatekeepers for the social work program. In this capacity, she is responsible for upholding social work standards and ensuring that students who are not yet competent do not pass the practicum until they have achieved the minimum standards (stated as learning goals and objectives) required by your social work program. Nevertheless, it may at times be difficult for her to assess a student as "unsatisfactory" because of the student's reaction, as well as the reactions of the practicum liaison and practicum director.

Naturally, the person most affected by the evaluation is you. You should not be too worried at the prospect of the mid-term evaluation conference because you will be warned beforehand if any disaster is about to befall you. However, you should prepare for the meeting with the same care as you prepare for your supervisory conferences. Look over your program's practicum evaluation form and your learning contract and decide how well you have achieved on the basis of documented evidence, that is, on the basis of written reports, process recordings, tapes, and so forth. You will then go into your evaluation conference prepared to absorb whatever feedback you receive. You will also be in a position to ensure that your lack of progress has been properly balanced with your triumphs.

The primary purpose of a mid-term practicum evaluation is to assess your achievements to date in order to focus and direct your future growth properly. One of your major tasks after the mid-term evaluation will be to revise your learning contract by paring down or supplementing some learning objectives and adding or eliminating others.

On occasion students are assigned an unsatisfactory rating. "Unsatisfactory" will follow only from unacceptable behavior or from some major problem that has persisted over time despite the efforts of the practicum instructor and student to solve it. In all likelihood your mid-term evaluation will prove to be nothing more than the completion of one more phases in your practicum experience.

We will now turn to some of the specific problem areas that you may encounter in your evaluation conference (Chapter Eight) and practicum termination (Chapter Nine). A few of them may already have arisen; some may not occur at all; and others may not appear until the second half of the practicum. You will probably not experience very many of them personally, but it is nevertheless useful for you to consider them.

EXERCISE 7.1: EVALUATING YOUR LEARNING AGREEMENT

Type: Application — Reflection

Purpose: To link theory, values, and knowledge with practice.

Exercise: The mid-term is a time not only to evaluate your practicum performance but also a time to review your learning opportunities. The way to accomplish this task is to review with your practicum instructor your learning agreement. Review your learning agreement and note the objectives you have not yet accomplished. Make concrete plans as to how you will accomplish these objectives. Identify other learning opportunities for the rest of your practicum experience.

Notes on Use

Student: Provide an example from your practice for each learning objective as described on the following pages. Use your notes and journal to find examples. Share with your practicum instructor. Are there areas you need to work on? Share your perceptions.

Practicum Instructor and *Practicum Tutorial Teacher:* Have students share examples of developing practice skills. Ask how they may improve in each area. What can students do for skills and competencies that require more assignments?

✔ *Developing a Professional Self.* Demonstrates a commitment to recognize values consistent with the NASW *Code of Ethics* or the applicable code. Includes demonstrating sensitivity and acceptance of human diversity on both a personal and professional level; addressing individual and systemic barriers related to racism, sexism, classism, anti-Semitism, ageism, ableism, and homophobia; recognizing, through critical self-reflection, the impact personal values and behaviors have on others; and meeting supervisory and placement policy and practice requirements.

Example:

✔ *Engaging.* Demonstrates the ability to consistently and effectively engage others: supervisor(s), team members, staff members, peers, resources, and consumer and client groups.

Example:

✔ *Contracting.* Utilizes effective communication and interview skills to clarify purpose and roles and to explore expectations in the process of establishing and maintaining a mutual contract with others: supervisor(s), team members, staff members, peers, resources, and consumer and client groups.

Example:

✔ *Assessing*. Demonstrates an understanding of person-in-environment perspective when collecting information from a variety of sources; identifying existing needs, strengths and priorities; organizing the information descriptively; and inviting collaborative analysis of issues/concerns with all those involved.

Example:

✔ *Planning*. Designs collaborative intervention plans incorporating the assessment; develops realistic goals that link interventions to the available services/resources; and articulates a rationale supporting these choices.

Example:

✔ *Implementing*. Demonstrates an ability to understand and articulate the theoretical rationale, as well as implement interventions, while monitoring both the process and progress of the intervention.

Example:

✔ *Documenting*. Documents in descriptive, measurable terms the process, progress, and outcomes in accordance with agency and social work practices.

Example:

✔ *Evaluating*. Demonstrates the ability to evaluate the effectiveness of the process, progress, outcomes, and services; and in so doing to invite, receive, and incorporate constructive feedback from supervisor(s), team members, staff, peers, resources, and consumer/client groups.

Example:

✔ *Terminating*. Consolidates and identifies the transferability of learning while recognizing, describing, and dealing effectively with issues of termination with supervisor(s), team members, staff, peers, resources, and consumer/client groups.

Example:

Name: _____

EXERCISE 7.2: AM I ON THE RIGHT ROAD?

Type: Reflection — Explanation

Purpose: To evaluate your learning to date.

Exercise: Rate the items on the following pages where 1 means "very unsatisfactory" and 5 means "very satisfactory."

Notes on Use

Student: After rating each item, rate the item in terms of where you want to be before your practicum ends. Discuss the items needing more work with your practicum instructor.

Practicum Instructor: Independently complete the ratings for your student. Discuss any differences.

Practicum Tutorial Teacher: Have students role-play the discussion of their evaluations where a different rating of performance is noted with their practicum instructors.

YOUR COMMUNITY:

✔ I have extended my knowledge and understanding of the geographic community and/or population that my agency and practicum setting serve.
   • Current rating_____
   • Specific activities that will improve my ability:

✔ I understand the significance and impact of the community and agency interaction.
   • Current rating_____
   • Specific activities that will improve my ability:

✔ I can identify gaps in and comprehend the relevant social welfare network and its ability to deliver services needed by my clients in a timely and integrated manner.
   • Current rating_____
   • Specific activities that will improve my ability:

✔ I am concerned about relevant community problems and am interested in taking whatever actions are possible and appropriate for myself as a representative of my agency and as a professional social worker.
   • Current rating_____
   • Specific activities that will improve my ability:

✔ I can evaluate the impact of significant community systems and resources or the lack thereof.
   • Current rating_____
   • Specific activities that will improve my ability:

YOUR AGENCY AND PRACTICUM SETTING:

✔ I have knowledge of my agency's and practicum setting's roles relative to the social welfare system and the target community and/or population.
  • Current rating_____
  • Specific activities that will improve my ability:

✔ I can function appropriately based on an understanding of my agency's and practicum setting's structures, politics, and programs.
  • Current rating_____
  • Specific activities that will improve my ability:

✔ I am able to interpret my agency's and practicum setting's purposes and programs to fellow professionals, to lay persons, and to clients with reasonable clarity and effectiveness.
  • Current rating_____
  • Specific activities that will improve my ability:

✔ I can evaluate the impact of my agency's and practicum setting's policies, programs, and resources as they affect outcome of service delivery.
  • Current rating_____
  • Specific activities that will improve my ability:

✔ Other_____
  • Current rating_____
  • Specific activities that will improve my ability:

WORK WITH CLIENT SYSTEMS AND SIGNIFICANT OTHERS:

✔ I am able to seek the information necessary for a person-in-environment assessment.
- Current rating_____
- Specific activities that will improve my ability:

✔ I am able to identify gaps in information and can differentiate between fact and inference.
- Current rating_____
- Specific activities that will improve my ability:

✔ I can form and maintain appropriate professional relationships with client systems that are client-system centered and purposeful.
- Current rating_____
- Specific activities that will improve my ability:

✔ I am able to explore problems, to elicit factors to enhance my understanding of clients' concern, and to assess clients' capacity and desire to change.
- Current rating_____
- Specific activities that will improve my ability:

✔ I am able to recognize client resources as well as personality and social factors that may contribute to the formation of problems.
- Current rating_____
- Specific activities that will improve my ability:

✔ I can facilitate a client system's utilization of external resources, and when appropriate, intervene directly on behalf of the client system.
   • Current rating_____
   • Specific activities that will improve my ability:

✔ I can appropriately utilize collaborative relationships with other systems on behalf of my client system.
   • Current rating_____
   • Specific activities that will improve my ability:

✔ I am able to synthesize perceptions and knowledge systematically in formulating an explicit assessment that I can substantiate with facts and support from theoretical premises.
   • Current rating_____
   • Specific activities that will improve my ability:

✔ I can establish, maintain, and manage an effective helping relationship with individuals, families, groups, and significant others.
   • Current rating_____
   • Specific activities that will improve my ability:

✔ I can differentiate between social and professional interchange and interact accordingly.
   • Current rating_____
   • Specific activities that will improve my ability:

✔ I can demonstrate empathy and use understandable language.
  • Current rating_____
  • Specific activities that will improve my ability:

✔ I can work with diverse groups by understanding and showing an appreciation for sociocultural, racial, ethnic, age, and gender differences as well as demonstrate an egalitarian value base.
  • Current rating_____
  • Specific activities that will improve my ability:

✔ I can suggest tasks and/or activities consonant with the ethnic and class lifestyles and practices of clients.
  • Current rating_____
  • Specific activities that will improve my ability:

✔ I can recognize and understand the significance of the termination process.
  • Current rating_____
  • Specific activities that will improve my ability:

✔ Other_____
  • Current rating_____
  • Specific activities that will improve my ability:

APPLICATION AND INTEGRATION OF
KNOWLEDGE WITH PRACTICE:

✔ I am able to recognize how personality, small group, family, organization, and sociocultural theory can be useful in explaining the meaning of behavior.
   • Current rating_____
   • Specific activities that will improve my ability:

✔ I am able to recognize the interplay of forces that create social problems and those that promote the resolution of problems and the impact all of this has on my clients.
   • Current rating_____
   • Specific activities that will improve my ability:

✔ I understand the function of advocacy and assume the role of advocate when appropriate.
   • Current rating_____
   • Specific activities that will improve my ability:

✔ I can identify the manifestations of racism, sexism, ageism, anti-Semitism, ableism, classism, heterosexism.
   • Current rating_____
   • Specific activities that will improve my ability:

✔ Other_____
   • Current rating_____
   • Specific activities that will improve my ability:

YOU AS A LEARNER:

✔ I can evaluate the effectiveness of my "use of self" throughout the intervention process.
- Current rating_____
- Specific activities that will improve my ability:

✔ I can effectively identify areas of my strength and weakness.
- Current rating_____
- Specific activities that will improve my ability:

✔ I effectively utilize the supervisory relationship of learning.
- Current rating_____
- Specific activities that will improve my ability:

✔ I respond to new knowledge thoughtfully and critically.
- Current rating_____
- Specific activities that will improve my ability:

✔ I demonstrate capacity for change in attitude.
- Current rating_____
- Specific activities that will improve my ability:

✔ I assume responsibility for my own learning.
- Current rating_____
- Specific activities that will improve my ability:

WORK MANAGEMENT AND PROFESSIONAL RELATIONSHIPS:

✔ I am reasonably prompt and responsible in making and keeping appointments, in planning for coverage, in carrying through on routines, and in ordering priorities toward effective use of my time.
   • Current rating_____
   • Specific activities that will improve my ability:

✔ I can follow through on the organization and management of assigned work.
   • Current rating_____
   • Specific activities that will improve my ability:

✔ I can write in understandable language, using correct sentence structure and grammar.
   • Current rating_____
   • Specific activities that will improve my ability:

✔ I demonstrate with staff an identification with my agency's and practicum setting's mission and a recognition of staff roles, appreciating some of the stresses inherent in them.
   • Current rating_____
   • Specific activities that will improve my ability:

✔ I can form and maintain appropriate relationships with colleagues and other personnel within my agency and practicum setting.
   • Current rating_____
   • Specific activities that will improve my ability:

✔ I am beginning to demonstrate the capacity to assume a professional role.
  • Current rating_____
  • Specific activities that will improve my ability:

✔ I can summarize and evaluate goals, interventions, and outcomes throughout the helping process.
  • Current rating_____
  • Specific activities that will improve my ability:

✔ Other_____
  • Current rating_____
  • Specific activities that will improve my ability:

✔ General Overall Comments:

Part Four

Summing It Up

THE FIRST CHAPTER in Part Four, Chapter Eight, is designed to help you deal with the unexpected that occurs along the way. It may be that bad weather ahead has forced a route change, it may be that you took a wrong turn and you need to backtrack a little, or you may find that you are on the wrong road altogether. Whatever the case, this chapter outlines some of the unexpected events that may occur.

Chapter Nine prepares you for this journey's end and starts you thinking about your next trip.

Chapter Eight

The hardest lesson I have learned is that I do have biases,
and my personal values cannot always be put aside.
My rule is: If forced with an ethical dilemma that I cannot
resolve with my own values, seek out help. Do not suffer alone!

— A Student

Which Way Do I Turn?

DILEMMAS, DILEMMAS, DILEMMAS...

MOST STUDENTS sail cheerfully through their practicums without ever encountering major roadblocks or hitting any potholes whatsoever. Occasionally, students encounter difficulties along the way that may require a minor change in the planned itinerary or possibly, a major rerouting. A few stumble into difficulties with their clients, with their practicum instructors, or with their classmates. They flounder sometimes through a lack of guidance or not thinking through the consequences of their actions and sometimes through sheer misfortune. Below are a few possible scenarios.

CLIENT-RELATED ISSUES

Clients assigned to beginning social work students are normally carefully selected so that the students will have a good chance of success and will not be overwhelmed by the nature of the clients' problems. Clients selected in this way have usually approached the practicum setting voluntarily, have a positive attitude toward social workers, and need a specific service that is easy to identify. Nevertheless, your practicum instructor may not be able to personally screen each of your clients, nor is there any guarantee that the screening process will be 100 percent effective. In short, the occasional inappropriate client may slip through.

Suppose that your initial interview with your first client goes something like the one presented in the following scenario.

Scenario One: Inexperience

You (with a welcoming smile): "Hello, Ms. Smith. My name is Martha Jones. I'm a social work student."

Ms. Smith (glaring grimly): "I don't want a student. I want someone who knows what he is doing."

Ms. Smith departs forthwith, ignoring your assurances that you may, in fact, be of some assistance to her, and you feel like finding a place to hide. You relate the incident to your practicum instructor, who supports you, finds another social worker for Ms. Smith, and gives you Ms. Brown instead. Ms. Brown looks, if anything, grimmer than Ms. Smith. After you have falteringly told her your name, you decide that you will not tell her you are a student until after you have established a rapport with her and have demonstrated your ability to help. Somehow, a suitable time for declaring your studenthood never arrives but, apart from that, the interview goes well. You write a triumphant process recording, glossing over the student bit by writing simply that you introduced yourself, and your practicum instructor congratulates you on your developing interviewing and relationship skills.

A week or so later, you are present as an observer at a community support group session which your practicum instructor is facilitating. There, to your horror, sits Ms. Brown. Your practicum instructor introduces you as a student. Ms. Brown sits up straight, piercingly fixes her eyes on you, and remarks that you never said you were a student. Your practicum instructor also gives you the piercing eye, and you spend the session in acute misery, paying practically no attention to what is going on. After the session, your practicum instructor is gentle with you because she remembers the Ms. Smith incident, but she also tells you quite definitely that your client had a right to know you were a student.

This said, your practicum instructor goes on to discuss the support group meeting, a discussion in which you are unable to participate intelligently because you were present only in body. You go home convinced that your practicum instructor thinks you are deceitful and naive and that Ms. Brown thinks just about the same. The result of this conviction is that your relationship with your practicum instructor deteriorates and your next interview with Ms. Brown is a bumbling disaster. You wonder if there is anything you can do to turn this situation around before it is irreparable.

Be honest with your clients, your practicum instructor, and yourself. Dilemmas will occur in many relationships and most anything can be revisited. You will need to get past your feelings of inadequacy or defensiveness and honestly assess what you can learn from this mistake. Turn it into a teachable moment, extract some learning value from it, and report this back to your practicum instructor. Discuss with her the best strategy for facing Ms. Brown and retrieving that relationship. The biggest hurdle is facing the dilemma, accepting responsibility for your part, and, most importantly, learning from it.

Scenario Two: Carelessness

Having learned from this incident, you immediately inform your third client, Mr. Green, that you are a student. He seems a little reluctant to talk, so you encourage him by giving your assurance that anything he says will be held in the strictest of confidence between the two of you. At the time, you believe this implicitly. Later, while you are talking to Doreen, the secretary, you realize that she is typing file records, including the information you obtained from Mr. Green. Later still, you learn that Mr. Green has asked for income assistance and your entry in his file has accordingly been shared with various government and law enforcement agencies. You think, with dismay, that you might as well have sent the record to the papers. Meanwhile, Mr. Green has discovered that what he said to you in the strictest confidence is now common knowledge in your local social service delivery system.

Filled with righteous indignation, Mr. Green complains to your practicum instructor. Your instructor explains to you that there is *absolute confidentiality*, where nothing your client says is shared with anyone in any form, and then there is *relative confidentiality*, where information is shared with colleagues as required. You will never be able to promise absolute confidentiality while you are still a student and, probably, you will never be able to promise it at all. Remember the *Code of Ethics* (Appendix A)?

Despite her gentleness, you feel that your practicum instructor is growing more and more convinced of your incompetence. You also feel vaguely resentful; she could have told you about relative confidentiality before. You look up confidentiality in your social work practice textbook and find the following principles:

✔ Do not discuss your clients outside the helping setting (e.g., office, class, group, meeting) even if you change the names or details. Discussing clients with family or friends is not permitted. The social work profession is often very stressful, and social workers sometimes need to "unwind" by talking about their feelings and the stress involved. Where such discussions involve clients, the discussion should take place at the office with supervisors and colleagues, not with family and friends who are not bound by the same rules of confidentiality as social workers. People may listen with interest to a social worker's story about her clients or her agency but, in the process, they may lose respect for the worker, the agency, or the profession. They may be thinking, "If I have a problem, I'll never go to her or any other social worker; it would get all over town."

✔ If a client is not at home when you call, leave only your first name and say nothing about the nature of your business.

✔ Do not become involved in formal discussions with colleagues over lunch or coffee. At a restaurant or other public place, there is obvious potential for your conversation to be overheard. Even when names are not mentioned, people might identify the client or think they have. Even if no identification is made, the nature of the discussion still gives others the impression that you are casual about confidentiality.

✔ Make arrangements for your telephone calls to be taken by someone else when you are interviewing a client. Interruptions lead to a break in rapport and to inadvertent breaches of confidentiality. To the client, the message may be, "She has more important things to do than listen to me."

✔ Ensure that your interview is private. It should be conducted in a private setting, not in the waiting room in view of other staff or clients.

✔ Do not leave case records, telephone messages, or rough notes on your desk. Case records often have the name of the client prominently displayed on the file and they may catch the eye of someone passing by. Put your records away before you leave your desk and make sure that client files are locked up overnight. If a client observes that you are haphazard in managing your files, he may assume, with some justification, that you will be haphazard in protecting what he tells you.

✔ Do not discuss clients at parties and other social activities. Colleagues often socialize together and, in such situations, it maybe very tempting to discuss a difficult case or talk about a case to illustrate a common problem.

✔ Even if your client seems unconcerned about confidentiality, respect it anyway. Your client may want to begin the interview in the waiting room or initiate or continue a discussion in a public place. In such circumstances, gently defer the discussion until you can arrange a private setting.

✔ The practicum setting dictates confidentiality regarding its internal operation. Your responsibility continues even after you have left your practicum.

Scenario Three: Personal Safety

Despite Mr. Green's indignation, your practicum instructor has decided that you should try to smooth matters over with him and continue to work with him. Your next contact with him is to be a home visit, and another student at your setting has been assigned to go with you for moral support. On the morning of the visit, Tim, the other student, tells you privately that he has urgent personal business to attend to and asks you if you would mind going by yourself. The practicum instructor need never know and it would help out Tim a lot.

You hesitate. You are away from home for the first time, living in a rural community when you are accustomed to city life. You selected a rural community because you had a theory that small towns were friendly, but this one seems to have closed its doors to outsiders. So far, you have not made many friends except for your classmates, your practicum instructor does not seem particularly impressed, and your clients have not liked you much either. The last thing you want to do, at this point, is to alienate Tim.

You run into your practicum instructor as you are leaving the office. She looks at your shoes, your suit, your makeup, hairstyle, and jewelry. Mr. Green, she points out tactfully, lives in a wooden frame house on a rutted dirt road in the middle of nowhere. Perhaps you would be more comfortable in different shoes and more casual attire, and in this way Mr.

Green might find you less threatening and intimidating . She adds that she thought Tim was going with you.

You tell her with some discomfort that Tim is meeting you in the parking lot and you will go home first to change your clothes. In fact, there is no time to change your clothes if you are not to be late for your appointment, and Tim is long gone looking after his affairs.

You are late anyway because road signs are few in the middle of nowhere and you had not believed that a road that bad would still be called a road. As you totter up the rickety steps to Mr. Green's front door, you notice that there is an outdoor toilet and a well with a hand pump a few hundred yards from the house. The implication strikes you slowly: no indoor bathroom, no running water in the house.

Mr. Green is more friendly toward you than you had expected. He ushers you into a room that appears to be carpeted with newspapers and dirty clothing. There is a wood stove in the corner with dangerous-looking pipes, a resident population of flies, and a smell whose origin you would rather not discover. Mr. Green removes a pile of something from an elderly sofa and invites you to take a seat.

He is far more communicative here than he was in the office. This house, he tells you with pride, has been in his family for four generations. He was born in it; he intends to die in it. You feebly try to follow why he introduced the thought of dying, Mr. Green, after all, is only 66 years old and he does not look suicidal. You notice he is looking at you and examining your total appearance, especially your legs.

You consider flight, telling yourself that you must have been mad to come here alone. However, Mr. Green is not actively leering, he is merely looking; and he is talking while he looks, approaching the subject of your visit. As you listen to him talk, he seems less a potential danger than a lonely, rather pathetic man. You are growing to understand him and his loneliness without family and friends.

You find yourself telling him about *your* lack of family and friends, enjoying his sympathy over your plight and his efforts to help you problem solve. In this same spirit of helpfulness, he offers you tea and homemade cake. You shudder inwardly but he would be very hurt it you refused and you decide to accept to preserve the relationship. You leave later than you had intended, basking in your new-found friendship.

There are several themes to this story. First, you were never in the slightest danger, but you might have been. Mr. Green might have fallen on your legs with lustful cries or you might have run into trouble on the road. *Never go alone into a potentially dangerous situation.* If a situation might be dangerous—for example, if you are a child protection worker called to a case where the alleged offender has a history of violent behavior—*request an escort*, preferably a police escort. You will serve humankind far more effectively if you first pay attention to ensuring your own safety.

Second, your clothes should be appropriate to your task. You should not wear city clothes on a rural visit any more than you should go to a staff or team meeting dressed in shorts, T-shirt, and sandals. Third, there is the matter of accepting food and drink. Many of the homes you enter as a social worker will not be clean by your standards and in many of them you will be offered something to eat. If cleanliness is not an issue, you may be allergic to some foods, or doubtful about ethnic variations, or simply afloat on the proffered sea of coffee. You need to develop non-offensive ways of refusing refreshments.

Fourth, your empathy with Mr. Green's friendless state led him to empathize with *your* friendless state so that your interview lost its focus and, before it was over, you had become the client. Sometimes it is helpful to divulge a little of your personal history to a client, but such a divulgence should be purposeful and focused on the client. It should never be used to gain an audience for your own woes. Neither should it reach the point where your client becomes the social worker and you become the client. Social workers have just as many woes as clients do—sometimes even the same woes—but the person to whom you can tell *your* tales of woe must be a relative, colleague, friend, or your own therapist, not an empathetic client.

Scenario Four: Learning Boundaries

Your practicum instructor has decided that, as well as continuing with Mr. Green, you should continue with Ms. Brown. Now that she knows you are a student, you are getting on extremely well with Ms. Brown. She has a mother aged 84, she tells you, who is recovering in the hospital after a heart attack. Her mother does not want to go to a nursing home after being discharged, but neither can she live alone as she used to do. It would probably be best, Ms. Brown says briskly, if she were to apply for legal guardianship of her mother and have her come to live with her. Touched by Ms. Brown's obvious concern for his mother's welfare, you agree.

Further probing reveals that Ms. Brown has a brother who is also prepared to look after their mother, but the brother's home would be totally unsuitable, Ms. Brown says. The brother's wife, "that Millie," has never gotten along with her mother-in-law. The brother's two boys are undisciplined horrors who would never give her a moment's peace. And anyway dear, Ms. Brown finishes comfortably, you know how it is with men. Imagine being bathed by a man, dear, you at 84 and helpless in the tub. Imagine being diapered by your son!

Since you have never seen an adult in diapers, you display a suitable degree of horror. You agree, a little reluctantly, to go with Ms. Brown to visit her mother and, if the mother consents, to appear in court on Ms.

Brown's behalf to obtain the legal guardianship. During your hospital visit, her mother consents quite cheerfully. You suspect that she would consent quite cheerfully to being dropped off the edge of a cliff, but this only reinforces in your mind the need for legal guardianship.

At this point, anxious about your impending court appearance, you approach your practicum instructor. Your practicum instructor draws a deep breath and clutches the edge of her desk. First, she says carefully, Ms. Brown's mother is not your client. Discharge planning for Ms. Brown's mother is the hospital's responsibility, and you must not interfere with someone else's responsibility unless you are specifically asked. Second, there appears to be a dispute among Ms. Brown, Ms. Brown's brother, and their mother.

You must not take sides in a family dispute, whether the issue is property, custody, guardianship, or anything else. Last but not least, if the legal guardianship question proceeds any further, it is not unlikely that Ms. Brown's brother will sue the agency, as well as you and/or your practicum instructor. You will not, therefore, appear in court. You will not see Ms. Brown again or Ms. Brown's mother or anyone having any connection at all with Ms. Brown. And in the future, you will check with your practicum instructor before you promise any client so much as a second cup of coffee. Your practicum instructor releases her breath as you release yours. You had no idea that a simple promise, kindly meant, could have so many dangerous ramifications.

The message here, of course, is that it is very easy to get in over your head through a sheer desire to be helpful. If you are not sure what you should promise to do for a client, promise nothing until you have asked your practicum instructor for advice.

Scenario Five: Emotions

Mr. Green does not appear for his next appointment, and you learn that he has been hospitalized with a stroke. You receive your practicum instructor's permission to visit him in the hospital and he seems pleased to see you and grateful for the visits. When he is due to be discharged, his social worker at the hospital asks for your input into the discharge planning. The medical staff is recommending a nursing home because Mr. Green is now partially paralyzed and can walk only with the help of a cane. Mr. Green, however, is mentally alert and has made it clear that he will not go into a nursing home. The next time you visit, he begs you to help him go home.

With Ms. Brown vividly in mind, you do not make any promises. You relay the conversation precisely to your practicum instructor and she commends you on your restraint. Nevertheless, it is apparent that a value conflict exists regarding the recommendation you will make to the discharge planning team. Your practicum instructor believes that Mr. Green will deteriorate and possibly die if he is allowed to go home. You believe that Mr. Green understands this.

If he chooses to die in his own home rather than live in a nursing home, it is his decision to make. Your practicum instructor argues that he may adapt to the nursing home better than he imagines, whereas, with all possible assistance, he would be unable to manage at home. It would be irresponsible, she says, to allow him to condemn himself without first giving the nursing home a try. You disagree. You think that he would never get out of the nursing home once he was in there and he would just die sooner and more miserably. Nevertheless, it is your practicum instructor's opinion that is relayed to the planning team, and their decision is the nursing home for Mr. Green.

The moral here is that sometimes you will disagree with a decision made by a team on behalf of your client. This is always painful. You may feel the urge to protest angrily and loudly, to write bitter letters, to make a scene, to withdraw from your practicum in disgust. However, none of these behaviors will help your present client and they will certainly jeopardize your ability to help your future clients. You can continue to function only by learning to cope rationally with decisions you believe to be wrong.

STUDENT-RELATED ISSUES

Not only will you run into client issues such as those just mentioned, but you may also run into dilemmas with other students as well. Consider the following scenario.

Scenario: Personal Boundaries

Your classmate, Karen, is a very religious and spiritual person. She makes no secret of the fact that she has been "born-again" and she wants others to share in her experience. One day she appears at work wearing a T-shirt with "Repent Your Sins" emblazoned on the back. She is called into the practicum instructor's office and emerges red-eyed and resentful because she has been told that her dress is inappropriate. She intends to protest to the instructor's supervisor and asks you, if you believe in religious freedom, to lend her your support.

First, suppose that you yourself are a born-again Christian. You agree with Karen's views, you consider it her duty to express her beliefs, and you have refrained from wearing such a shirt only because you know your practicum instructor would disapprove and you have enough tension already. You therefore go with Karen to the supervisor's office. There you are told quite firmly that you are entitled to your own beliefs but so are other people. Some clients and some staff, too, may be offended by the shirt. Since social workers have a particular duty to avoid imposing their personal values on other people, Karen should not wear the shirt or any similar shirt again. If the behavior persists, further action will have to be taken.

You and Karen carry your complaint to your practicum liaison with similar results. Karen does not wear the shirt again and the incident passes. However, you are left with the feeling that it is now you and Karen against the world. Social work, you think, is definitely an environment that pays lip service to tolerance while accepting, in fact, only the most conventional of behaviors.

Now suppose that you are not a born-again Christian. You do not share Karen's views but you believe she has the right to express them and you go with her to the practicum instructor's office. You discover, once more, that a social worker's right to self-expression is limited. If you do not support Karen, for whatever reason, you may find the relationship strained. You stand to lose an important component of your practicum: the student support system.

The issue here, of course, is a social worker's right to express religious, political, or sexual beliefs that others may find deviant. Topics such as homosexuality, abortion, extramarital relationships, communism, and a whole variety of other "isms" are all potentially explosive. Issues that are not explosive at all to the majority culture may conjure sparks within minority groups. Social workers are not personally more or less tolerant than members of other professions.

Some social workers blithely accept just about everything; others hold deep-seated and sometimes rigid views about the moral acceptability of this or that. The difference between a social worker and a member of another profession is that the social worker is required to be non-judgmental with clients. Social work is done within the client's belief system, from the client's point of view, toward the client's ends. If the social worker does not happen to agree with the client, she has to carefully consider how she communicates this while respecting the client's point of view. She must not impose her own views on the client. You must never disrupt the helping process by pushing your own beliefs or agenda.

T-shirts bearing slogans, badges, buttons, crests, some types of clothing, and even some hairstyles carry a message about the wearer's own beliefs. Such messages may not be given by a social worker to a client; therefore, it follows that a social worker in the workplace is more limited than other people in the matter of dress and general freedom of expression. It is a strange paradox that increased tolerance for the client's freedom of expression leads to a reduced tolerance for the social worker's freedom of expression. It may seem odd that the social work world demands more conventional behavior from its inhabitants than do other worlds *because* of its need to be tolerant.

INSTRUCTOR-RELATED ISSUES

You may also run into dilemmas with your practicum instructor. Consider the following two scenarios.

Scenario One: Power

So far, your relationship with your practicum instructor has had its ups and downs. To add to your problems, Tim was seen by a client in the shopping mall when he was supposed to have gone with you to visit Mr. Green. Somehow, the news reached your practicum instructor, who immediately confronted you. She noted the fact that you had told her a direct untruth and then she explained at length about solitary excursions turning into potentially dangerous situations. You do not know what she said to Tim, but he was irritated for at least a couple of days.

When your practicum instructor tells you that she will be out of town for the following week, you breathe a soft sigh of relief. Another backup instructor whom you do not like very well has meanwhile been assigned to help you with any problems that may arise. You are determined that none will arise but, in fact, one does. You find yourself discussing this problem over lunch with a third worker whom you like much better than the one who was assigned to you. He gives you good advice and you do not bother to discuss the problem with your backup practicum instructor or with your regular practicum instructor when she returns.

A week later, when you have another minor problem, you wander into your mentor's office. Again, he gives you good advice and, again, you do not bother to take the problem to your practicum instructor. You continue asking him about your difficulties for another month until the situation comes to your practicum instructor's attention.

It is apparent at first glance that she is angry. She reminds you of the occasion when you accompanied Karen to her supervisor's office. You did not discuss the T-shirt issue with her first; you did not air your own feelings about it or give her the opportunity to explain why she thought that Karen's dress was inappropriate. Instead, you went immediately to her supervisor.

Now, you have established a habit of taking your difficulties to another staff member without also sharing them with your practicum instructor. Do you see that she cannot do her job as your practicum instructor unless she is aware of your problems and unless there is frank communication between the two of you? What are your feelings on this matter?

Your first feeling is bewilderment. You asked for advice, informally, from a person you liked; you did this in part because you had a desire to appear competent in the eyes of your practicum instructor. You wanted to appear to have solved your problems on your own, and you wanted to make up for past mistakes by coming up with a good performance. You see your practicum instructor's point of view but you privately think that she is overreacting.

There are two issues here. The first is the hierarchical structure of your practicum setting and the second is the continuity of your learning experience.

By now, you will have looked at your agency's organizational chart. In every agency, there are lines of authority, usually passing from the board of directors to the executive director to department heads to supervisors within the departments to front-line workers. Roles, responsibilities, and limits of decision-making authority are carefully defined. Formal lines of communication are set up to control and facilitate the passage of information. Moreover, the importance of information should not be underestimated. By far, information is the most important tool that any administrator can possess, from the lowliest front-line worker to the chairperson of the board.

When you went to your practicum instructor's supervisor without first consulting her, you broke two rules: jumping over established lines of authority and depriving your practicum instructor of information. When you asked advice from another social worker without your practicum instructor's knowledge, you broke the same rules.

There are times when you will work quite legitimately with social workers other than your practicum instructor. On these occasions, however, your practicum instructor will *know*. She probably will have assigned the worker you are to work with; she will have planned the projects you are involved with; she will have discussed any problems with you and the other social worker. Thus her authority is in no way undermined and her information system is left intact.

If you remember the two key words, *authority* and *information*, you should be able to avoid potential problems with your practicum instructor and other workers. Remember, too, that authority is particularly precious to those who have very little. Some social workers assigned to work with you may have no supervisees. They may want especially to be informed before the fact of anything you are going to discuss with your practicum instructor; and it is common courtesy to inform them.

The second issue has to do with the continuity of your learning. You should realize by now that learning in your practicum is not a random matter. It has been carefully planned by you and your practicum instructor so that your learning objectives will be reached in phases, one experience building on another and leading on to a third. Furthermore, your planned practice experiences are designed to fit with the theoretical material you have learned in the classroom. The minimum standards set by your social work program underpin the material taught in the classroom. Your practicum learning goals and objectives, as well, are drawn from the program's minimum standards and in this way the connection between theory and practice is established.

Your practicum instructor is your guide on this planned path of learning. If she is not kept fully informed about your experiences, your problems, and your achievements, she cannot guide you and you cannot learn. Moreover, not all social workers are qualified to be practicum instructors. Your mentor, during the month or so you asked him for advice, did not mention to your practicum instructor that he was advising you. He, too, crossed the lines of authority and information in his attempt to be helpful.

Scenario Two: Emotional Boundaries

Throughout your school life thus far, you have been supported by your parents. Recently, however, your father lost his job and his financial contribution to you has diminished by a substantial amount. You have been obliged to take a part-time job to make ends meet; you arrive at your practicum already tired with another endless day ahead. Your performance and even your interest in your performance have dropped to unsatisfactory levels.

Your practicum instructor confronts you with her perception of your failing efficiency. Do you agree with her estimate? Is anything wrong? Is there anything she can do to help? You agree wholeheartedly with her estimate but you do not want to discuss your personal problems with her. You feel your relationship is not good enough for that. Neither do you want to discuss them with your practicum liaison, whom you do not know well, and there is no one else you feel you can approach. You drag helplessly on and you finish, as you suspected you might, with some "unsatisfactory" mid-term practicum ratings.

Many students have personal problems that interfere in relatively small ways with their practicum performances. Problems in the areas of money, transportation, failed romances, or family stresses are not uncommon. For some students, however, personal problems can prove to be overwhelming; they threaten their practicum settings and possibly their entire social work careers. Your practicum instructor is not in a position to intrude in your personal life. The most she can do is to point out your work deficiencies and stand by ready to help you if she is asked. Your practicum liaison is in the same position; in fact, she is in a worse position because she is not present in your practicum setting to monitor the sequence of events.

However reluctant you may be to disclose your personal affairs, it may be better for you to do so than to risk an unsatisfactory rating. Neither your practicum instructor nor your liaison want to see you fail. They will do everything in their power to help you out of your difficulty and arrange the practicum to suit your needs, without prying, with the very minimum of intrusion. Often, all you need to do is ask.

SUMMARY

Ideally, you will never encounter any of the situations we discussed, but reading about possibilities will enable you to be more sensitive to variations of the themes described. Problems may arise around your clients, your practicum instructor, other staff, or other students in your practicum. There may also be personal difficulties that detract quite noticeably from your professional performance.

Some students do not like to admit that they are students. Perhaps, if you are older, you do not feel comfortable in the student role and avoid any mention of the fact out of sheer embarrassment. If age is not a factor, you may feel that a client who knows you are a student will not accept you, or a colleague will not believe you are competent. Skipping the "I am a student" part when you introduce yourself may not appear to be a major blunder. However, it is tantamount to misrepresentation, and misrepresentation *is* a major blunder. It is illegal for you to make claims about yourself or your services that are inaccurate or cannot be substantiated. And you make such a claim by omission when you fail to say you are a social work student and allow clients to assume that you are a qualified social worker.

Beginning social workers sometimes promise clients that "anything you say will never go beyond this room." In fact, information about clients is commonly typed by secretaries and is shared with agency staff, staff from other social service agencies, and various government and law enforcement bodies. It is therefore untrue and unethical to promise a client *absolute* confidentiality. The most you can do is to ensure *relative* confidentiality by guarding your files, watching what you say and where you say it, and giving out information only to those who need it to serve the client.

Courting danger in pursuit of providing service to clients is neither selfless nor noble—it is merely foolish. You should not go alone into any situation that is potentially dangerous. Whether the danger exists, of course, is a matter of judgment. Your practicum instructor may have a number of reasons for asking you to take a companion, none of which is connected with danger. Perhaps she wants another student or a worker to observe your interview; perhaps two students are to be involved with the same client. Nevertheless, if you are supposed to go with someone, go with someone. Do not go alone.

Social workers have the same needs as clients for sympathy and sharing. The helping relationship, by its very nature, involves an unusual degree of closeness, and it is easy, in the midst of this closeness, to create a confusion between helper and client. Any sharing of your personal life with a client must be purposeful and intended for the benefit of your client.

Some clients are good at manipulating social workers, particularly beginning social workers who are inexperienced in the art of manipulation. You may be persuaded to involve yourself with another worker's client. You may find that you have inadvertently taken sides in a family dispute. Such situations can create conflicts between social workers, between agencies, and with clients. In the worst case, the client, or a relative of the client, may take legal action against the individual worker and/or the agency. It pays, therefore, to inform your practicum instructor about your involvement every step of the way.

Sometimes decisions regarding your client are not made by you alone, but by a team. You may be tempted to make an emotional protest if the team reaches a decision with which you do not agree. Such behavior will not help your present client and may jeopardize your ability to help future clients. The social work world is relatively rigid with regard to codes of behavior, dress, and even expression. The reason for this is not that social workers as a group are less tolerant than other people; rather, social workers must take particular care not to impose their values on their clients. Some forms of dress or behavior make a clear value statement and thus are discouraged in the social work environment.

If you are to maintain good relationships with your practicum instructor and other workers within your practicum setting, it is important for you to respect established lines of authority and communication. Respect for your practicum instructor's position will also help to ensure that your learning proceeds along a planned path. Practice goals based on theory will be achieved in easy stages, each experience designed to build on the one before it.

Occasionally, a personal crisis may disrupt your learning process. It may be difficult for you to disclose your personal problems to your practicum instructor or practicum liaison, but, if you can bring yourself to do so, they will probably do everything in their power to help you and will intrude only minimally into your affairs.

We will now turn to the last phase of your practicum experience, the termination process.

Name: _____

EXERCISE 8.1: ASKING FOR DIRECTIONS

Type: Application

Purpose: To apply knowledge of ethical dilemmas regarding confidentiality to hypothetical situations.

Exercise: Discuss the issue of confidentiality with your practicum instructor using each of the case vignettes on the following pages. Before the discussion, write your comments in the space provided following each vignette.

Notes on Use

Student: Read each vignette and apply the principles of confidentiality to describe what you would do in the situation. Discuss this with your practicum instructor and/or other students and consider if, on the basis of those discussions, you could do anything differently or an addition to what you described.

Practicum Instructor: Ask your student to describe how he or she would respond to each vignette; share your point of view and how you might respond.

Practicum Tutorial Teacher: Have students share their responses with each other through small group discussions. See if there is a general consensus on what might be the most ethical action for each vignette.

VIGNETTE ONE

An adult client confides in you about a mutual genital exploration with an 11-year-old boy. There have been no complaints from the boy or from his parents. There is no evidence that such behavior was engaged in except for the information supplied by your client. Is there a need for you to document what the client told you? Remember, there is a possibility that someone else will be reading this file.

✔ As a student, I would. . .

✔ After discussing this with others, I would. . .

VIGNETTE TWO

At a hospital setting, in a medical team conference, you are discussing a case of a 24-year-old woman who is undergoing tests to determine the cause of and treatment for her inability to become pregnant. Prior to going back to school, you were employed in child protection services and knew the patient when she was 16 or 17 years old. You remember that at that time she had several VD infections. The patient recognizes you. She does not want her "past to be disclosed" and asks you to "maintain confidentiality." What can you do?

✔ As a student, I would. . .

✔ After discussing this with others, I would. . .

VIGNETTE THREE

You are late handing in a process recording to your practicum instructor. You also do not have time to drive the recording over to your practicum setting. You suddenly remember the fax machine at the School of Social Work and decide this is the most expedient way to have your process recording reach your practicum instructor. You fax 12 pages to your practicum instructor. To your surprise, you discover the next day that she has never received it. So you fax it again. This time she receives it but calls you urgently to meet with her. You have kept all client name and identifying information throughout the recording. The recording was left in the open area of the fax room and others could have read the material. There is no indication as to where the first fax went and who might have received it. Have you failed to maintain confidentiality of your clients? What do you do? What should happen?

✔ As a student, I would. . .

✔ After discussing this with others, I would. . .

Name: _____

EXERCISE 8.2: DETOURS AND BACKTRACKING

Type: Reflection

Purpose: To consider the dilemmas you have faced and reflect on your responses to them.

Exercise: What ethical dilemmas have you had to deal with in your present practicum setting? How were they resolved? Write your comments in the space provided.

Notes on Use

Student: Select one dilemma in each of the areas of client system–related, student-related, and instructor-related dilemmas. Describe what happened and what you did. Reflect on the outcome and what you might do differently if you had it to do over again.

Practicum Instructor: Share with your students a dilemma in any one of the three categories listed and model your reflection of what you did, how it turned out, and why you chose that response. Ask your students to share their experiences with similar dilemmas.

Practicum Tutorial Teacher: In small groups, have your students describe one of their dilemmas and as a group, reflect on what occurred, the outcome, and how it might have been handled differently.

CLIENT SYSTEM–RELATED DILEMMAS:

✔ What happened:

✔ What action you took:

✔ What you might do differently:

STUDENT-RELATED DILEMMAS:

✔ What happened:

✔ What action you took:

✔ What you might do differently:

INSTRUCTOR-RELATED DILEMMAS:

✔ What happened:

✔ What action you took:

✔ What you might do differently:

CULTURAL-RELATED DILEMMAS:

✔ What happened:

✔ What action you took:

✔ What you might do differently:

AGENCY-RELATED DILEMMAS:

✔ What happened:

✔ What action you took:

✔ What you might do differently:

OTHER DILEMMAS:

✔ What happened:

✔ What action you took:

✔ What you might do differently:

Chapter Nine

Who says termination is a grieving process? While I'll be sad to say goodbye to my practicum, I am really looking forward to graduating and taking with me everything I have learned. I know that I can't stop here though. I will need to be on top of all the new knowledge that comes out for years.

— A Student

Leaving and Linking

I N A SENSE, YOU HAVE BEEN PREPARING for leaving your practicum from the first day you walked into it. Everyone knew from the very beginning that you would only be there for a specified period of time, such as a semester or two. You knew. Your practicum instructor knew and she assigned clients to you on that understanding. Any projects you were involved in were likely designed so that they could be completed in the time available.

Nevertheless, terminating your practicum is complex because it is dictated by a date set by your program, not necessarily by the readiness of your clients, the completion of the work you set out to accomplish, or even your own sense of readiness to depart. These factors make leaving the practicum somewhat complicated and difficult. There is a sadness to every ending, even if it is mingled with a feeling of accomplishment. You are saying goodbye to people, a place, a phase of your life—ending a journey.

Not only are the rituals that you must go through with regard to closure and evaluation practically useful, they should also provide you with a sense of completion, of things having ended right. You need to think about leaving your clients, your practicum instructor, and your practicum setting. You need to think about this, especially in regards to your clients—the meaning and impact your leaving will have on them, as well as the effect on you.

LEAVING YOUR CLIENTS

Every session you have with a client involves a termination phase. About 10 minutes before the interview is due to end, you tell your client that 10 minutes remains, you deal with unfinished business, you summarize the session, and you make arrangements for the next one. A similar process takes place if you are bringing closure to a group as the leader or facilitator, or ending a meeting as the chair or resource person.

Termination of a helping relationship—whether it has been therapeutic, educational, or developmental; voluntary or mandated; focused on personal growth, social control, community development, or societal change; involved individuals, groups, or entire communities—follows the same process. There is usually some discussion of the ending right from the start, but as the end approaches there is more discussion and preparations are made for the actual termination. Progress is reviewed and plans are made. Often there is some type of ritual or formality to mark this ending.

The client still has a life and may possibly still have a problem. If client-related practice objectives have not been achieved or new ones come to light, your client may need to be referred either to a different agency or to another worker within your practicum setting. In either case, you will need to summarize your client's progress to date so that the new worker will understand the situation and can assess whether the referral is appropriate. It is also courteous to speak personally with the worker to whom you have made the referral. Even if there is no referral, you will need to prepare a closing summary to share with your client and to enter in his or her file.

For example, Ms. Smith's elusive problem may finally have been defined as an inability to manage her budget, compounded by a tendency to spend the rent money on marijuana. At your suggestion, Ms. Smith enrolled in a drug rehabilitation program. For a month or two, all seemed well. Ms. Smith arrived at every interview with a lined sheet of paper ruled neatly into "income" and "outgo," accompanied by receipts, none of them for the purchase of marijuana.

Then, a chance remark by Jane, her 7-year-old daughter, revealed the fact that Ms. Smith had recently acquired a number of boyfriends.

Confronted, Ms. Smith agreed that a friend she met in the drug rehabilitation group had shown her how to supplement her income. The budget was balanced, Ms. Smith said cheerily. She was happy; Jane, properly fed and clothed for the first time in years, was also happy; and the boyfriends were especially happy.

You are not as happy, but by now you have developed an affection for Ms. Smith, with her toothy smile and her balanced budget. She, on her part, regards you as the only person in her life who knows she is a prostitute, knows she does drugs, and still recognizes her as a concerned mother and a worthwhile person. She does not perceive that she has a problem any more, but she still likes to come and talk. When you leave, she says, she will probably stop coming; it would not be the same with anyone else.

You think that she probably will stop coming even though you have referred her to another social worker. In your care, she has progressed from supporting her habit with the rent money to supporting it through prostitution, but you are still reluctant to let her go. You like her—you will miss her. In a strange way you are almost as dependent on her as she is on you.

An experienced worker will usually be able to prevent a client from becoming dependent on a helping relationship and will be able to avoid becoming dependent on a client. A beginning worker, anxious to establish empathy, is more likely to slide into a comfortable though unproductive mutually dependent relationship. It is just as well that your relationship with Ms. Smith will end because you are leaving; but the termination of any long-term helping relationship will always have difficult elements.

For example, reactions commonly associated with loss—denial, anger, sadness, guilt, relief, abandonment—can be experienced by both clients and students. Feelings both you and your clients have had about previous endings are likely to be reactivated. Managing the impending endings and feelings related to past losses is a challenging experience for students. It requires time and the ability to sort out both personal reactions and issues related to your own process of termination with the needs and concerns of your clients.

One of the things you can do is warn your clients well beforehand, to give them plenty of time to adjust to the idea and gradually reduce the frequency of their visits. For example, instead of seeing Ms. Smith weekly, you might see her once every two weeks and then once every three weeks. Right from the outset you need to discuss with clients your status as a student and the time frame of the practicum, which introduces the issue of termination at the beginning. This way it will not be new information at the end of the practicum.

During the last session, you can summarize with Ms. Smith how far she has come and what problems remain to be resolved, and introduce her to her new social worker. If she is to terminate with the agency, you can tell her that she is welcome to return if the need arises. Few agencies conduct follow-up interviews with clients because of limited resources but, ideally, a contact several weeks after official termination and another a few months later is a good idea.

It is important to be aware of the tendency to avoid or deny the ending process. Your practicum instructor can help you be alert to the difficulties you may have in terminating with clients and finishing projects but remember there will also be feelings and issues related to ending your relationship with your practicum instructor.

LEAVING YOUR
PRACTICUM INSTRUCTOR

Terminating with your practicum instructor formally begins with your final evaluation conference. It is very similar to the preliminary and mid-term evaluations discussed in previous chapters of this book. The exercises at the end of this chapter will help you summarize and synthesize your learning.

Your relationship with your practicum instructor may have been excellent, indifferent, or relatively poor—depending on the circumstances and your and her individual qualities. Whatever the relationship, you owe it to her to sit down with her at the end of your practicum and review what went right and what went wrong, and what would have been a helpful alternative.

When you leave she will probably have another social work student. She will be able to teach this student more effectively if she receives quality feedback from you about how well you thought she functioned in her teaching role. Also, your social work program may require you to evaluate your practicum instructor's performance and your practicum experience as part of the termination process.

Other programs assume, much more informally, that you will provide feedback in the same way that feedback was also provided to you. Some of the many criteria upon which you can provide feedback to your practicum instructor include the dimensions presented in Exercise 9.1 found at the end of this chapter.

Discussing the ending of your relationship with your practicum instructor gives you an avenue for exploring your feelings and issues about leaving. Reviewing your progress through the use of oral and written evaluations provides an opportunity for both of you to identify the highlights, low points, and areas for future development.

The difficult part about this is that your practicum instructor's evaluation of you, her judgment, and opinions regarding your abilities can have a fairly major impact your future. Hopefully this issue has been addressed previously—that you have learned how to share your views and hear hers and have found a way to balance the ideal of reciprocity and mutuality with her authority and power.

A central issue in the evaluation has to do with fairness. The question, "Was it fair?" is not asking whether it was negative. Unfair evaluations may be positively glowing; fair evaluations may be glowing or disastrous. When you answer the question about the fairness of your practicum instructor's evaluation of your progress within your practicum, you should ask yourself whether her comments were specific enough to be useful and whether they were documented with reference to your work. However objective she tries to be and however much documentary evidence she tries to produce, some parts of your practicum evaluation will still rest on her own perceptions. For example, she may write, "Betty feels she is not accepted by agency staff, whereas, in reality, staff members both like and accept her." Unless you can accurately survey the attitudes of agency staff, you cannot know objectively which is the correct perception. There should not be many remarks on your formal evaluation that are purely a matter of perception, particularly if they are negative remarks.

Other aspects to review in relation to your practicum instructor, as your practicum comes to an end, are the ways in which conflict was managed, the impact of her teaching style on your learning, and your satisfaction with the degree of autonomy. These aspects are important considerations as you think about linking your practicum to future endeavors.

Reviewing Your Disagreements

You will have had a very dull and unusual practicum if you have not disagreed at all with your practicum instructor. Disagreements in some areas are normal, almost inevitable, and often productive. For example, in the last chapter, you thought that Mr. Green should be allowed to return to his own home after his stroke and your practicum instructor thought that he should go to a nursing home. Earlier in your practicum you may have found it difficult to disagree with your practicum instructor—the power balance, after all, is unequal—but this time, on Mr. Green's behalf, you were prepared to stand your ground. You argued rationally, logically, and sometimes passionately; your practicum instructor countered; and in the end it was her opinion that prevailed.

Whether or not this conflict was resolved depends on how you felt about losing. Resolution does not necessarily mean that one of you must change sides and agree with the other; there are many conflicts which, in this sense, can never be resolved. Resolution does mean that, if you cannot agree, you can amicably agree to disagree.

Teaching Style

Reflecting on your autonomy as learner as well as on the degree of direction or structure you need will add to your ability to link this practicum to other learning experiences. Naturally, you will need more guidance during the first practicum than you will during subsequent ones. You can expect your independence at the beginning to be limited. Your practicum instructor must find a reasonable balance between dogging your every step and allowing you complete autonomy. The optimum balance will vary with the individual, depending on each student's inclinations and abilities. Essentially, you must give a subjective estimate of how comfortable you felt with the degree of freedom you were allowed.

Did you feel suffocated or rootless or free within secure limits? Did your practicum instructor assign you every task, ignoring your attempts to find tasks for yourself? Did she welcome or stifle your bids for independence? Was she responsive to your suggestions? Was she over-controlling and anxious or uncomfortably permissive?

Did your practicum instructor's teaching methods make allowance for your learning styles? (Learning styles have already been discussed in Chapter Five.) If you learn best through active experimentation, for example, and your practicum instructor expected you to learn through reading and talking things out, you may have experienced frustration.

Remember, when answering the question, that your practicum instructor could not take your learning style into account if you did not tell her what it was. If you did tell her, and she was still unable to provide you with appropriate learning experiences, this fact is worthy of note.

Making Recommendations

Your evaluative comments about your practicum instructor will be taken seriously by your practicum liaison, your practicum instructor, your practicum director, and your practicum setting. All comments, if reinforced by other students over time, will have an eventual effect on whether your practicum instructor continues as a practicum instructor and, possibly, on whether the practicum setting continues to have students. More students may be assigned, or fewer, or none, or a different type of student.

You have a responsibility to your program, your practicum setting, and your practicum instructor to give as honest an evaluation as possible. An honest evaluation should also be constructive. If you have a negative comment to make, add recommendations as to how the situation might be improved—balance the negatives with positives.

LEAVING YOUR AGENCY AND PRACTICUM SETTING

Before you leave your practicum setting, you will say your goodbyes to people you have met, particularly those whom you have worked with closely. You should not automatically assume that it is goodbye forever. Social work is a small world and it is likely that you will meet these people again, possibly very soon or in future years. If you part on a positive note, not only will you feel better about your practicum experience, you will have made an investment in your social work career.

Planning an event to mark the end of the practicum is a useful way of acknowledging the relevance of the experience for both you, your practicum instructor, and the staff in the practicum setting. You will probably be asked to evaluate your practicum setting in the same way you were asked to evaluate your practicum instructor.

Reviewing your experience in the practicum setting can help you make linkages to other settings, management structures, and types of social service delivery systems. All of this information will assist you in making informed decisions about where you go or what you do next. Even the physical layout of this setting might have an influence on the type of physical surroundings you will chose if the opportunity arises. Aspects that are helpful to review include the place and role of students, the learning opportunities and the appropriateness of the workload, and the degree to which the practicum setting was able to meet your learning goals.

The Place and Role of Students

One aspect in evaluating your practicum setting is the attitude of the social workers and staff toward social work students. Did they accept you, want you, like you, or did you feel marginalized? If you did feel marginalized, make a particular effort to decide whether it was your student status or something else going on in the setting.

Factors other than acceptance should also be taken into account. Did other social workers cheerfully use you like a workhorse, assuming you were there to do whatever no one else had time for? If they did, that is flattering in its way. At least they thought you were competent. But it also shows a lack of understanding of your student role. If they did understand that you were there to learn, did they contribute to your learning? Did they willingly answer your questions, offering information and adding explanations? Did they suggest that you accompany them to noon lectures, special presentations, or other events approved by your practicum instructor? Did they appear concerned if you sat in a corner reading?

Your assessment of the social workers' attitudes will necessarily be subjective. Accordingly, you should be very careful that you have not read into a look or a gesture something that was never there. Reading in a practicum setting seems sometimes to be associated with a certain amount of guilt. Other social workers are not reading; they are not even sitting; they are dashing hither and thither in a flurry of activity. You may have felt that it was lazy to sit down with a book, but reading is a way to learn, and learning is why you were there.

It will be important for you to clear with your practicum instructor if it is all right to read at your practicum and what reading material is appropriate. Sometimes students read for their classroom courses while they are at their practicums. This may or may not be acceptable to the practicum instructor. Some do not mind if the reading materials are directly related to the practicum setting or the client's problem, but they do not approve of reading general classroom assignments.

Attitude is also a factor in providing assistance in times of crisis. The definition of a crisis depends on who is doing the defining. You may have thought you were in a crisis and resented the fact that nobody ran to your aid. On the other hand, your perception is that a crisis is still a crisis and it is not unreasonable to expect that someone will take the time to explain to you why things are not as bad as you thought.

There are three things to consider when thinking about assistance in a crisis. First, did you know whom to ask, failing the presence of your practicum instructor? Second, did the person you asked respond to your satisfaction at the time? Third, looking back at the situation, do you think that the response was adequate given the actual nature of the crisis? If you did not know where to go for help or if you received inadequate help, these things are worthy of mention.

Learning Opportunities and the Appropriateness of the Workload

Think about the range of learning opportunities in your practicum setting. In terms of quantity and quality of learning opportunities, did the available assignments and projects provide you with different types of learning? In answering this question you are essentially evaluating your practicum setting as an environment for field education learning. What learning opportunities were available to you in terms of number and type of cases and exposure to different situations?

Was your workload heavy, light, or satisfactory? The optimum size of a workload depends on a number of factors. First, how many other activities were you involved in? If casework was only a part of your total learning experience, two or three cases may well have been a satisfactory load. Remember, what is good for one social work student may not be good for another.

How complex were the cases assigned? Some cases may have demanded a great deal of attention, both in terms of analyzing and planning and in terms of the number of contacts required. Other cases, on the other hand, may have needed only a few contacts and involve fairly routine provision of material assistance.

At what level were you required to explore and document your cases? For example, you may have been asked to prepare a client treatment plan for each one, listing key facts, the projected feelings of all significant persons, possible behavioral manifestations of feelings, desired goals including time frames, measurements for practice-related objective achievement, selection of various intervention strategies, and conditions of their implementation.

Additionally, you may have been asked to incorporate a single-subject research design into each case, with an analysis of results and a final report. You may have been asked for a written analysis of each taped interview and a process recording for each interview that was not taped. Of course, being requested to do all this is highly unlikely. Nevertheless, some practicum instructors prefer that you study a few cases thoroughly rather than work with a number at a more superficial level. This determination will be up to your practicum instructor.

Your estimate of your workload will depend on how well you were able to cope with it. If you had difficulty, you will probably say it was heavy; if you were comfortably occupied, you will say it was satisfactory. This is as good a way to do it as any, but you should also take into account the speed at which you work. Do you think, for example, that you work faster than average and that another student, given your satisfactory caseload, might have found it too heavy? Perhaps you had an integrative seminar or group conference that gave you some basis for comparison of yourself with other students in their practicums.

Accomplishments

Were you able to accomplish your learning goals and objectives? Your responses here will probably be that you accomplished some objectives fully and others to a certain extent. If there are definite reasons why you were not able to accomplish some learning objectives to the degree you would have liked, you should try to identify whether your practicum set any blocks or barriers to learning. You may have been blocked in your desire to learn about work with children because your setting did not have the facilities to provide a playroom. You may have been blocked in your desire to practice couple counseling because it was your practicum instructor's policy to assign only individual clients to beginning students.

All practicum settings have limitations, and you should have been aware of most of them before you set your learning goals and objectives. For example, if you had a strong desire to observe work with children and you had a setting that did not provide such interventions, you can hardly blame the setting for blocking the achievement of your objective. On the other hand, some limitations are not apparent until you are actually in the setting. Perhaps you carefully established that your practicum setting provided couple counseling but you did not know that, as a beginning social work student, you would not be allowed to practice it.

Finally, it is useful for you to think about the degree to which you were satisfied with your overall learning experience. Would you recommend this practicum setting to future social work students? Why or why not? Is it more suitable for some types of students than others?

Evaluating your practicum setting is important information as you leave the setting and begin to plan for your future learning needs. In addition, evaluation provides important information that both the practicum setting and the practicum director need for ongoing planning, development, and monitoring of practicums for student learning.

PREPARING FOR YOUR NEXT PRACTICUM

At the beginning of this chapter, when we discussed termination with clients, we mentioned that the termination phase normally includes making arrangements for the following session. In the same way, termination of the first practicum involves making plans for the second one (if appropriate), and termination of the second one involves making plans for entering the workforce.

If your social work program has a second practicum, it will be different from the first in that you will not be starting from the very beginning. You now have some skills, some practical knowledge, and a clearer idea of where you are going. In a way, you pose a greater challenge to your second practicum instructor as a higher-level student since she cannot now assume that you know nothing. She must assess your existing skills and knowledge before she can know what assignments will be appropriate for you.

You can help your next practicum instructor in this task if you complete your own self-evaluation at the end of your first practicum. You will have to do this anyway to prepare yourself for your final evaluation, but now you can take it one step further. You can write down not just what you have achieved in this first practicum but what you would like to achieve in the second. In other words, you can start to tentatively formulate your learning goals and objectives and begin to write your second learning agreement.

Of course, these goals and objectives will have to be revised to conform to the nature of the second practicum setting; however, you will have a guide. You will have written down, while they are still fresh in your mind, the learning goals and objectives you have reached and the goals you have not yet reached, your strengths, your weaknesses, and your preferred methods of learning. You will have prepared a beginning map to your overall professional career. In fact, you may already have some thoughts about the type of practicum setting or workplace that may best meet your future educational needs.

The Trip of a Lifetime

To thrive as a professional social worker and enjoy the journey as well, somewhere along the way you need to learn to take care of yourself. You may have put your own stuff on hold, put your needs on the back burner, or given up your aerobics class in order to get through the term. But you cannot do that forever or you will eventually succumb to the professional malaise of burnout.

Burnout is the result of emotional and physical exhaustion and is a reaction to an unhealthy amount of stress over time. You may have encountered burned out professionals in your practicum setting. They are the ones who are cynical, are negative, have few positive feelings for clients, and have little faith in their (or anyone's) ability to effect change. They are not the best role models for you, but they can alert you to what can happen if you don't find ways to relieve the pressure, cope with the stress, and have a little fun in your chosen career.

Social work is a challenging profession. You have undoubtedly experienced glimpses of the frustrations inherent in those challenges but hopefully you have also experienced the sense of satisfaction in facing those challenges, making a difference, and accomplishing something—even a little thing. A career in social work can last you a lifetime as the profession offers such variety and scope. And there are many things you can do to keep it interesting but not overwhelming.

It is important that you exercise your body and your mind. Having physical outlets such as hiking, jogging, biking, or walking on a regular basis is an important part of self-care. Similarity, being a lifelong learner will exercise your mind. Attending continuing professional education workshops or courses, reading professional journals, and even becoming a practicum instructor yourself are ways to stimulate your brain and prevent burnout. Making connections with others and developing a trusting network and support system will go a long way to making social work an enjoyable career choice. You also need to find ways to have some fun, to laugh, and to think positively. Setting realistic goals, learning how to manage your time, and taking time out to "exhale" are strategies that will enable you to find fulfillment in the profession of social work.

We hope you will continue to use the metaphor of a journey as you look back to where you have been, take stock of where you are now, and look ahead to where you will be traveling next. Hopefully you will use some of the exercises throughout your career in times when you want to explore, reflect, or apply what you are learning to what you are doing. May your travels be rewarding!

SUMMARY

Ending your practicum involves terminating with your clients, your practicum instructor, and your practicum setting as a whole.

Tell your clients well in advance that you will be leaving in order to give them time to prepare psychologically. It is sometimes advisable to reduce the frequency of your contacts toward the end—seeing them once every three or four weeks, for example, instead of every week. During the last session, you can summarize how far your client has come and what problems remain to be solved. You can also introduce the new worker if your client is to remain with the agency or discuss the transfer to a new agency if your client has been referred.

You owe it to your practicum instructor to sit down with her at the end of the practicum to review her performance. You may be required to fill out a practicum instructor evaluation form and she, like you, will not want any surprises.

A good practicum instructor should be available and approachable. She should also have a sound knowledge base and be able to direct your learning in ways that will facilitate the achievement of your goals. She should know what teaching methods are likely to be effective in light of your preferred learning styles and she should be able to evaluate fairly how much you have learned. Evaluation is ongoing and should be provided in the form of quality feedback at each supervisory conference session. The mid-term and final evaluations will then be only a formal summary of what has been said before.

Disagreement between you and your practicum instructor in some areas is normal and often productive. However, conflicts involving deeply felt opinions must be resolved if the relationship is to be preserved. In some cases, it will not be possible to reach agreement, and resolution will come only through an agreement to disagree.

A good practicum instructor will allow you as much independence as possible, taking into account your abilities and the vulnerability of your clients. Expectations of your performance will be set at a level that is generally consistent with the standards of other practicum instructors.

Preparation for your final evaluation will include completing a self-evaluation. You can use this self-evaluation to formulate tentative learning goals for your second practicum or for a work experience. In addition to formulating tentative list of learning goals, you will have the advantage next time of knowing a little more about what you want from a practicum. You will be a little less anxious because you have been through it all before. You will have the skills and practical knowledge to enable you to move on to a satisfying and gratifying career in social work.

We hope you have truly enjoyed your practicum and that this book has contributed to that enjoyment. Good luck with your next learning experience!

NOTES ON CHAPTER NINE:

Name: _____

EXERCISE 9.1: HOW WAS YOUR TOUR GUIDE? EVALUATION OF YOUR INSTRUCTOR

Type: Reflection — Application

Purpose: To reflect on your practicum instructor's approach and teaching style and share your perspective of her abilities.

Exercise: By considering each of the aspects of your practicum instructor's abilities listed on the following pages, you will produce a useful synthesis of your perceptions and experiences, which you can then use to provide feedback to her.

Notes on Use

Student: Reflect on your entire practicum process and try to respond honestly and specifically using examples as much as possible.

Practicum Instructor and *Practicum Tutorial Teacher:* Ask your students to provide feedback and encourage them to share with you some or all they wrote in this exercise. Discuss in detail.

✔ Availability of your practicum instructor:

✔ Your practicum instructor's knowledge base:

✔ Your practicum instructor's ability to link knowledge and practice:

✔ Your practicum instructor's choice of assignments in terms of relevance of tasks, cases, and projects:

✔ Your practicum instructor's ability to reinforce your strengths:

✔ Your practicum instructor's ability to identify areas for your improvement and communicate them to you:

✔ Your practicum instructor's ability to challenge you to be reflective and self-critical:

Name: _____

EXERCISE 9.2: HOW WAS THE LANDSCAPE?
EVALUATION OF YOUR PRACTICUM SETTING

Type: Reflection

Purpose: To reflect on your experience and the strengths and limitations of the practicum setting.

Exercise: What would you want future students to know about this practicum setting?

Notes on Use

Student: Complete the following questionnaire and hand it in to the practicum office for the benefit of the practicum director and future students.

Practicum Instructor and *Practicum Tutorial Teacher:* Using the questions on the next page, give your appraisal of the practicum settings with which you are familiar. This will be helpful feedback for the practicum director and may be useful to prospective students.

✔ Would you recommend this practicum setting for future social work students? (Why or why not?)

✔ What should a student know before beginning a practicum in your setting?

✔ What advice can you give prospective students to enhance their learning and ensure success?

Name: _____

EXERCISE 9.3: THINKING ABOUT YOUR NEXT JOURNEY

Type: Reflection

Purpose: To explore your future learning needs.

Exercise: Identify five personal qualities that you have noticed from your practicum experience that you would like to continue to build upon—for example, your use of appropriate humor, or sense of justice, etc. Identify two personal qualities that you would like to moderate—for example, being overly nervous around authority, or procrastination in writing reports. Record these for planning toward your next practicum setting.

Notes on Use

Student: Take into account your personal attributes at this point in your professional development as an ongoing process. Be honest with yourself. Look back to Chapters One and Two. Have you changed? Was the change expected?

Practicum Instructor: Refer back to Chapters One and Two and discuss with the student the changes you have observed.

Practicum Tutorial Instructor: This is you last opportunity to give your student some feedback that can be brought forward to the next learning experience.

QUALITIES I WANT TO CONTINUE TO DEVELOP:

✔

✔

✔

✔

✔

QUALITIES I WANT TO CHANGE:

✔

✔

✔

✔

Name: _____

EXERCISE 9.4 RECHARGING YOUR BATTERIES

Type: Reflection

Purpose: To reward yourself for hard work.

Exercise: Treat yourself to a positive reward for a successful journey—for example, a nice dinner, a short vacation, a present.

Notes on Use

Student, Practicum Instructor, and *Practicum Tutorial Teacher:* You deserve a positive reward. Treat yourself to something nice and enjoy. Good luck.

Appendixes

Appendixes

THE FIRST APPENDIX, Appendix A, is the NASW's current *Code of Ethics.* Since you must pursue ethical practice while you are in your practicum, we thought it would be advantageous for you to read it early in your practicum experience.

The second appendix, Appendix B, presents a simple mid-term and final evaluation form that you can use if your program does not have one. It can be modified to suit your learning needs.

Appendix A

THE SOCIAL WORKER'S CONDUCT AND COMPORTMENT
AS A SOCIAL WORKER

THE SOCIAL WORKER'S ETHICAL RESPONSIBILITY
TO CLIENTS

THE SOCIAL WORKER'S ETHICAL RESPONSIBILITY
TO COLLEAGUES

THE SOCIAL WORKER'S ETHICAL RESPONSIBILITY
TO EMPLOYERS AND EMPLOYING ORGANIZATIONS

THE SOCIAL WORKER'S ETHICAL RESPONSIBILITY
TO THE SOCIAL WORK PROFESSION

THE SOCIAL WORKER'S ETHICAL RESPONSIBILITY
TO SOCIETY

NASW's Code of Ethics

STANDARDS AND ETHICS TO LIVE AND PRACTICE BY

THE SOCIAL WORKER'S CONDUCT AND COMPORTMENT AS A SOCIAL WORKER

Propriety

The social worker should maintain high standards of personal conduct in the capacity or identity as social worker.

- The private conduct of the social worker is a personal matter to the same degree as is any other person's, except when such conduct compromises the fulfillment of professional responsibilities.

- The social worker should not participate in, condone, or be associated with dishonesty, fraud, deceit, or misrepresentation.

- The social worker should distinguish clearly between statements and actions made as a private individual and as a representative of the social work profession or an organization or group.

Competence and Professional Development

The social worker should strive to become and remain proficient in professional practice and the performance of professional functions.

- The social worker should accept responsibility or employment only on the basis of existing competence or the intention to acquire the necessary competence.

- The social worker should not misrepresent professional qualifications, education, experience, or affiliations.

Service

The social worker should regard as primary the service obligation of the social work profession.

- The social worker should retain ultimate responsibility for the quality and extent of the service that the individual assumes, assigns, or performs.

- The social worker should act to prevent practices that are inhumane or discriminatory against any person or group of persons.

Integrity

The social worker should act in accordance with the highest standards of professional integrity and impartiality.

- The social worker should be alert to and resist the influences and pressures that interfere with the exercise of professional discretion and impartial judgment required for the performance of professional functions.

- The social worker should not exploit professional relationships for personal gain.

Scholarship and Research

The social worker engaged in study and research should be guided by the conventions of scholarly inquiry.

- The social worker engaged in research should consider carefully its possible consequences for human beings.

- The social worker engaged in research should ascertain that the consent of participants in the research is voluntary and informed without any implied deprivation or penalty for refusal to participate, and with due regard for participants' privacy and dignity.

- The social worker engaged in research should protect participants from unwarranted physical or mental discomfort, distress, harm, danger, or deprivation.

- The social worker who engages in the evaluation of services or cases should discuss them only for professional purposes and only with persons directly and professionally concerned with them.

- Information obtained about participants in research should be treated as confidential.

- The social worker should take credit only for work actually done in connection with scholarly and research endeavors and credit contributions made by others.

THE SOCIAL WORKER'S ETHICAL RESPONSIBILITY TO CLIENTS

Primacy of Clients' Interests

The social worker's primary responsibility is to clients.

- The social worker should serve clients with devotion, loyalty, determination, and the maximum application of professional skill and competence.

- The social worker should not exploit relationships with clients for personal advantage, or solicit the clients of one's agency for private practice.

- The social worker should not practice, condone, facilitate, or collaborate with any form of discrimination on the basis of race, color, sex, sexual orientation, age, religion, national origin, marital status, political belief, mental or physical handicap, or any other preference or personal characteristic, condition, or status.

- The social worker should avoid relationships or commitments that conflict with the interests of clients.

- The social worker should under no circumstances engage in sexual activities with clients.

- The social worker should provide clients with accurate and complete information regarding the extent and nature of the services available to them.

- The social worker should apprise clients of their risks, rights, opportunities, and obligations associated with social service to them.

- The social worker should seek advice and counsel of colleagues and supervisors whenever such consultation is in the best interest of clients.

- The social worker should terminate service to clients, and professional relationships with them, when such service and relationships are no longer required or no longer serve the clients' needs or interests.

- The social worker should withdraw services precipitously only under unusual circumstances, giving careful consideration to all factors in the situation and taking care to minimize possible adverse effects.

- The social worker who anticipates the termination or interruption of service to clients should notify clients promptly and seek the transfer, referral, or continuation of services in relation to the clients' needs and preferences.

Rights and Prerogatives of Clients

The social worker should make every effort to foster maximum self-determination on the part of clients.

- When the social worker must act on behalf of a client who has been adjudged legally incompetent, the social worker should safeguard the interests and rights of that client.

- When another individual has been legally authorized to act on behalf of a client, the social worker should deal with that person always with the client's best interest in mind.

- The social worker should not engage in any action that violates or diminishes the civil or legal rights of clients.

Confidentiality and Privacy

The social worker should respect the privacy of clients and hold in confidence all information obtained in the course of professional service.

- The social worker should share with others confidences revealed by clients, without their consent, only for compelling professional reasons.

- The social worker should inform clients fully about the limits of confidentiality in a given situation, the purposes for which information is obtained, and how it may be used.

- The social worker should afford clients reasonable access to any official social work records concerning them.

- When providing clients with access to records, the social worker should take due care to protect the confidences of others contained in those records.

- The social worker should obtain informed consent of clients before taping, recording, or permitting third party observation of their activities.

Fees

When setting fees, the social worker should ensure that they are fair, reasonable, considerate, and commensurate with the service performed and with due regard for the clients' ability to pay.

- The social worker should not divide a fee or accept or give anything of value for receiving or making a referral.

THE SOCIAL WORKER'S ETHICAL RESPONSIBILITY TO COLLEAGUES

Respect, Fairness, and Courtesy

The social worker should treat colleagues with respect, courtesy, fairness, and good faith.

- The social worker should cooperate with colleagues to promote professional interests and concerns.

- The social worker should respect confidences shared by colleagues in the course of their professional relationships and transactions.

- The social worker should create and maintain conditions of practice that facilitate ethical and competent professional performance by colleagues.

- The social worker should treat with respect, and represent accurately and fairly, the qualifications, views, and findings of colleagues and use appropriate channels to express judgments on these matters.

- The social worker who replaces or is replaced by a colleague in professional practice should act with consideration for the interest, character, and reputation of that colleague.

- The social worker should not exploit a dispute between a colleague and employers to obtain a position or otherwise advance the social worker's interest.

- The social worker should seek arbitration or mediation when conflicts with colleagues require resolution for compelling professional reasons.

- The social worker should extend to colleagues of other professions the same respect and cooperation that is extended to social work colleagues.

- The social worker who serves as an employer, supervisor, or mentor to colleagues should make orderly and explicit arrangements regarding the conditions of their continuing professional relationship.

- The social worker who has the responsibility for employing and evaluating the performance of other staff members should fulfill such responsibility in a fair, considerate, and equitable manner, on the basis of clearly enunciated criteria.

- The social worker who has the responsibility for evaluating the performance of employees, supervisees, or students should share evaluations with them.

Dealing with Colleagues' Clients

The social worker has the responsibility to relate to the clients of colleagues with full professional consideration.

- The social worker should not solicit the clients of colleagues.

- The social worker should not assume professional responsibility for the clients of another agency or a colleague without appropriate communication with that agency or colleague.

- The social worker who serves the clients of colleagues, during a temporary absence or emergency, should serve those clients with the same consideration as that afforded any client.

THE SOCIAL WORKER'S ETHICAL RESPONSIBILITY TO EMPLOYERS AND EMPLOYING ORGANIZATIONS

Commitments to Employing Organization

The social worker should adhere to commitments made to the employing organization.

- The social worker should work to improve the employing agency's policies and procedures, and the efficiency and effectiveness of its services.

- The social worker should not accept employment or arrange student field placements in an organization which is currently under public sanction by NASW for violating personnel standards, or for imposing limitations on or penalties for professional actions on behalf of clients.

- The social worker should act to prevent and eliminate discrimination in the employing organization's work assignments and in its employment policies and practices.

- The social worker should use with scrupulous regard, and only for the purpose for which they are intended, the resources of the employing organization.

THE SOCIAL WORKER'S ETHICAL RESPONSIBILITY TO THE SOCIAL WORK PROFESSION

Maintaining the Integrity of the Profession

The social worker should uphold and advance the values, ethics, knowledge, and mission of the profession.

- The social worker should protect and enhance the dignity and integrity of the profession and should be responsible and vigorous in discussion and criticism of the profession.

- The social worker should take action through appropriate channels against unethical conduct by any other member of the profession.

- The social worker should act to prevent the unauthorized and unqualified practice of social work.

- The social worker should make no misrepresentation in advertising as to qualifications, competence, service, or results to be achieved.

Community Service

The social worker should assist the profession in making social services available to the general public.

- The social worker should contribute time and professional expertise to activities that promote respect for the utility, the integrity, and the competence of the social work profession.

- The social worker should support the formulation, development, enactment, and implementation of social policies of concern to the profession.

Development of Knowledge

The social worker should take responsibility for identifying, developing, and fully utilizing knowledge for professional practice.

- The social worker should base practice upon recognized knowledge relevant to social work.

- The social worker should critically examine, and keep current with, emerging knowledge relevant to social work.

- The social worker should contribute to the knowledge base of social work and share research knowledge and practice wisdom with colleagues.

THE SOCIAL WORKER'S ETHICAL RESPONSIBILITY TO SOCIETY

Promoting the General Welfare

The social worker should promote the general welfare of society.

- The social worker should act to prevent and eliminate discrimination against any person or group on the basis of race, color, sex, sexual orientation, age, religion, national origin, marital status, political belief, mental or physical handicap, or any other preference or personal characteristic, condition, or status.

- The social worker should act to ensure that all persons have access to the resources, services, and opportunities which they require.

- The social worker should act to expand choice and opportunity for all persons, with special regard for disadvantaged or oppressed groups and persons.

- The social worker should promote conditions that encourage respect for the diversity of cultures which constitute American society.

- The social worker should provide appropriate professional services in public emergencies.

- The social worker should advocate changes in policy and legislation to improve social conditions and to promote social justice.

- The social worker should encourage informed participation by the public in shaping social policies and institutions.

NOTES ON APPENDIX A:

Appendix B

INTRODUCTION

LEARNING GOAL 1: FUNCTIONS EFFECTIVELY WITHIN A PROFESSIONAL CONTEXT

LEARNING GOAL 2: FUNCTIONS EFFECTIVELY WITHIN AN ORGANIZATIONAL CONTEXT

LEARNING GOAL 3: FUNCTIONS EFFECTIVELY UTILIZING KNOWLEDGE-DIRECTED PRACTICE SKILLS

LEARNING GOAL 4: FUNCTIONS EFFECTIVELY WITHIN AN EVALUATIVE CONTEXT

*I hated to be evaluated but I knew it was necessary
to protect future clients from inadequate social workers.*

— A Student

Sample Evaluation Form

STUDENT'S NAME: _____

AGENCY _____

PRACTICUM SETTING: _____

PRACTICUM INSTRUCTOR: _____

PRACTICUM LIAISON: _____

PRACTICUM TUTORIAL TEACHER: _____

MID-TERM OR FINAL EVALUATION (circle one)

DATE: _____

INTRODUCTION

This simplified generic practicum evaluation form has been devised to provide a guide for the mid-term and final evaluation of your student's performance in the practicum. The following four learning goals have been selected for the evaluation (you may add, modify, or delete any of them—they are only examples):

- Functions effectively within a professional context

- Functions effectively within an organizational context

- Functions effectively utilizing knowledge-directed practice skills

- Functions effectively within an evaluative context

It is intended that this form will serve as an evaluation guide for students in the practicum. Your student should have a copy of this form at the outset of the practicum and should be encouraged to use it for self-evaluation throughout the entire course.

In addition, it is expected that the practicum instructor and practicum liaison will use this evaluation form for ongoing assessment as well as for mid-term and final evaluations of the student's performance in the practicum.

Although the completion of the evaluation form is expected to be a cooperative effort between the student and practicum instructor, the practicum instructor is ultimately responsible for rating, documenting, and summarizing the student's performance.

Feedback

The practicum instructor, practicum liaison, and student are requested to conjointly discuss and examine each learning objective and provide an example of how the objective was achieved and an example of how it was not achieved (if appropriate).

LEARNING GOAL 1:
FUNCTIONS EFFECTIVELY WITHIN
A PROFESSIONAL CONTEXT

The student will develop an understanding of the profession of social work and will demonstrate both professional development and an ability to function within a professional framework. This includes articulating and applying knowledge and values within a generalist social work framework.

Learning Objectives

1.1 Has demonstrated an understanding of the "person-in-environment" concept from a social work perspective.

How demonstrated:

How not demonstrated:

Specific areas that need improvement:

On a scale from 1 to 5, rate the practicum student in relation to this specific learning objective where 1 means "complete failure" and 5 means "complete success." Student Rating: _____

What specific tasks and/or behaviors need to be demonstrated to raise the above rating on the next practicum evaluation? Explain in detail below:

1.2 Has demonstrated values consistent with those of the profession and an understanding of and commitment to ethical standards.

How demonstrated:

How not demonstrated:

Specific areas that need improvement:

On a scale from 1 to 5, rate the practicum student in relation to this specific learning objective where 1 means "complete failure" and 5 means "complete success." Student Rating: _____

What specific tasks and/or behaviors need to be demonstrated to raise the above rating on the next practicum evaluation? Explain in detail below:

1.3 Has demonstrated the ability to engage in a variety of social work roles.

How demonstrated:

How not demonstrated:

Specific areas that need improvement:

On a scale from 1 to 5, rate the practicum student in relation to this specific learning objective where 1 means "complete failure" and 5 means "complete success." Student Rating: _____

What specific tasks and/or behaviors need to be demonstrated to raise the above rating on the next practicum evaluation? Explain in detail below:

1.4 Has demonstrated the ability to recognize the impact of personal behaviors and values on others.

How demonstrated:

How not demonstrated:

Specific areas that need improvement:

On a scale from 1 to 5, rate the practicum student in relation to this specific learning objective where 1 means "complete failure" and 5 means "complete success." Student Rating: _____

What specific tasks and/or behaviors need to be demonstrated to raise the above rating on the next practicum evaluation? Explain in detail below:

1.5 Has demonstrated the ability to take initiative toward increasing knowledge and skills relevant to performance demands.

How demonstrated:

How not demonstrated:

Specific areas that need improvement:

On a scale from 1 to 5, rate the practicum student in relation to this specific learning objective where 1 means "complete failure" and 5 means "complete success." Student Rating: _____

What specific tasks and/or behaviors need to be demonstrated to raise the above rating on the next practicum evaluation? Explain in detail below:

1.6 Has demonstrated the ability to utilize field instruction appropriately by active participation and preparation.

How demonstrated:

How not demonstrated:

Specific areas that need improvement:

On a scale from 1 to 5, rate the practicum student in relation to this specific learning objective where 1 means "complete failure" and 5 means "complete success." Student Rating: _____

What specific tasks and/or behaviors need to be demonstrated to raise the above rating on the next practicum evaluation? Explain in detail below:

1.7 Has demonstrated the ability to meet work performance requirements in the practicum, including punctuality and productivity.

How demonstrated:

How not demonstrated:

Specific areas that need improvement:

On a scale from 1 to 5, rate the practicum student in relation to this specific learning objective where 1 means "complete failure" and 5 means "complete success." Student Rating: _____

What specific tasks and/or behaviors need to be demonstrated to raise the above rating on the next practicum evaluation? Explain in detail below:

1.8 Other_____

How demonstrated:

How not demonstrated:

Specific areas that need improvement:

On a scale from 1 to 5, rate the practicum student in relation to this specific learning objective where 1 means "complete failure" and 5 means "complete success." Student Rating: _____

What specific tasks and/or behaviors need to be demonstrated to raise the above rating on the next practicum evaluation? Explain in detail below:

LEARNING GOAL 2: FUNCTIONS EFFECTIVELY WITHIN AN ORGANIZATIONAL CONTEXT

The student will articulate an understanding of, and an ability to work within, a social service organization according to its purpose, structure, and constraints and to analyze the relationship to the community served.

Learning Objectives

2.1 Has demonstrated the ability in the practicum setting to work within and interpret policies, structures, and functions to clientele and others.

How demonstrated:

How not demonstrated:

Specific areas that need improvement:

On a scale from 1 to 5, rate the practicum student in relation to this specific learning objective where 1 means "complete failure" and 5 means "complete success." Student Rating: _____

What specific tasks and/or behaviors need to be demonstrated to raise the above rating on the next practicum evaluation? Explain in detail below:

2.2 Has demonstrated the ability to identify and link available services, resources, and opportunities to meet the needs of the client system.

How demonstrated:

How not demonstrated:

Specific areas that need improvement:

On a scale from 1 to 5, rate the practicum student in relation to this specific learning objective where 1 means "complete failure" and 5 means "complete success." Student Rating: _____

What specific tasks and/or behaviors need to be demonstrated to raise the above rating on the next practicum evaluation? Explain in detail below:

2.3 Has demonstrated the ability to describe and analyze the relationship between agency policies and service delivery.

How demonstrated:

How not demonstrated:

Specific areas that need improvement:

On a scale from 1 to 5, rate the practicum student in relation to this specific learning objective where 1 means "complete failure" and 5 means "complete success." Student Rating: _____

What specific tasks and/or behaviors need to be demonstrated to raise the above rating on the next practicum evaluation? Explain in detail below:

2.4 Has demonstrated the ability to understand the broad social issues facing the organization and the community.

How demonstrated:

How not demonstrated:

Specific areas that need improvement:

On a scale from 1 to 5, rate the practicum student in relation to this specific learning objective where 1 means "complete failure" and 5 means "complete success." Student Rating: _____

What specific tasks and/or behaviors need to be demonstrated to raise the above rating on the next practicum evaluation? Explain in detail below:

2.5 Other_____

How demonstrated:

How not demonstrated:

Specific areas that need improvement:

On a scale from 1 to 5, rate the practicum student in relation to this specific learning objective where 1 means "complete failure" and 5 means "complete success." Student Rating: _____

What specific tasks and/or behaviors need to be demonstrated to raise the above rating on the next practicum evaluation? Explain in detail below:

LEARNING GOAL 3:
FUNCTIONS EFFECTIVELY UTILIZING
KNOWLEDGE-DIRECTED PRACTICE SKILLS

The student will apply knowledge to practice situations and develop competence in applying the general method of social work.

Learning Objectives for Engagement

3.1 Has demonstrated the ability to engage others and identify problems or concerns.

How demonstrated:

How not demonstrated:

Specific areas that need improvement:

On a scale from 1 to 5, rate the practicum student in relation to this specific learning objective where 1 means "complete failure" and 5 means "complete success." Student Rating: _____

What specific tasks and/or behaviors need to be demonstrated to raise the above rating on the next practicum evaluation? Explain in detail below:

3.2 Has demonstrated the ability to clarify purpose, role, and establish a mutual contract.

How demonstrated:

How not demonstrated:

Specific areas that need improvement:

On a scale from 1 to 5, rate the practicum student in relation to this specific learning objective where 1 means "complete failure" and 5 means "complete success." Student Rating: _____

What specific tasks and/or behaviors need to be demonstrated to raise the above rating on the next practicum evaluation? Explain in detail below:

3.3 Other_____

How demonstrated:

How not demonstrated:

Specific areas that need improvement:

On a scale from 1 to 5, rate the practicum student in relation to this specific learning objective where 1 means "complete failure" and 5 means "complete success." Student Rating: _____

What specific tasks and/or behaviors need to be demonstrated to raise the above rating on the next practicum evaluation? Explain in detail below:

Learning Objectives for Assessment

3.4 Has demonstrated the ability to identify the necessary data required and obtain it from appropriate sources.

How demonstrated:

How not demonstrated:

Specific areas that need improvement:

On a scale from 1 to 5, rate the practicum student in relation to this specific learning objective where 1 means "complete failure" and 5 means "complete success." Student Rating: _____

What specific tasks and/or behaviors need to be demonstrated to raise the above rating on the next practicum evaluation? Explain in detail below:

3.5 Has demonstrated the ability to articulate a comprehensive assessment.

How demonstrated:

How not demonstrated:

Specific areas that need improvement:

On a scale from 1 to 5, rate the practicum student in relation to this specific learning objective where 1 means "complete failure" and 5 means "complete success." Student Rating: _____

What specific tasks and/or behaviors need to be demonstrated to raise the above rating on the next practicum evaluation? Explain in detail below:

3.6 Other_____

How demonstrated:

How not demonstrated:

Specific areas that need improvement:

On a scale from 1 to 5, rate the practicum student in relation to this specific learning objective where 1 means "complete failure" and 5 means "complete success." Student Rating: _____

What specific tasks and/or behaviors need to be demonstrated to raise the above rating on the next practicum evaluation? Explain in detail below:

Learning Objectives for Planning

3.7 Has demonstrated the ability to develop a social work plan based on the assessment.

How demonstrated:

How not demonstrated:

Specific areas that need improvement:

On a scale from 1 to 5, rate the practicum student in relation to this specific learning objective where 1 means "complete failure" and 5 means "complete success." Student Rating: _____

What specific tasks and/or behaviors need to be demonstrated to raise the above rating on the next practicum evaluation? Explain in detail below:

3.8 Other_____

How demonstrated:

How not demonstrated:

Specific areas that need improvement:

On a scale from 1 to 5, rate the practicum student in relation to this specific learning objective where 1 means "complete failure" and 5 means "complete success." Student Rating: _____

What specific tasks and/or behaviors need to be demonstrated to raise the above rating on the next practicum evaluation? Explain in detail below:

Learning Objectives for Implementation

3.9 Has demonstrated the ability to identify and select appropriate helping strategies.

How demonstrated:

How not demonstrated:

Specific areas that need improvement:

On a scale from 1 to 5, rate the practicum student in relation to this specific learning objective where 1 means "complete failure" and 5 means "complete success." Student Rating: _____

What specific tasks and/or behaviors need to be demonstrated to raise the above rating on the next practicum evaluation? Explain in detail below:

3.10 Has demonstrated an understanding of the complexities and difficulties in change.

How demonstrated:

How not demonstrated:

Specific areas that need improvement:

On a scale from 1 to 5, rate the practicum student in relation to this specific learning objective where 1 means "complete failure" and 5 means "complete success." Student Rating: _____

What specific tasks and/or behaviors need to be demonstrated to raise the above rating on the next practicum evaluation? Explain in detail below:

3.11 Other_____

How demonstrated:

How not demonstrated:

Specific areas that need improvement:

On a scale from 1 to 5, rate the practicum student in relation to this specific learning objective where 1 means "complete failure" and 5 means "complete success." Student Rating: _____

What specific tasks and/or behaviors need to be demonstrated to raise the above rating on the next practicum evaluation? Explain in detail below:

Learning Objectives for Evaluation

3.12 Has demonstrated the ability to analyze and describe different phases of the helping process.

How demonstrated:

How not demonstrated:

Specific areas that need improvement:

On a scale from 1 to 5, rate the practicum student in relation to this specific learning objective where 1 means "complete failure" and 5 means "complete success." Student Rating: _____

What specific tasks and/or behaviors need to be demonstrated to raise the above rating on the next practicum evaluation? Explain in detail below:

3.13 Has demonstrated the ability to involve the clients in evaluating the extent to which the objectives are being accomplished.

How demonstrated:

How not demonstrated:

Specific areas that need improvement:

On a scale from 1 to 5, rate the practicum student in relation to this specific learning objective where 1 means "complete failure" and 5 means "complete success." Student Rating: _____

What specific tasks and/or behaviors need to be demonstrated to raise the above rating on the next practicum evaluation? Explain in detail below:

3.14 Other_____

How demonstrated:

How not demonstrated:

Specific areas that need improvement:

On a scale from 1 to 5, rate the practicum student in relation to this specific learning objective where 1 means "complete failure" and 5 means "complete success." Student Rating: _____

What specific tasks and/or behaviors need to be demonstrated to raise the above rating on the next practicum evaluation? Explain in detail below:

Learning Objectives for Termination

3.15 Has demonstrated the ability to terminate constructively with appropriate follow-up or referral.

How demonstrated:

How not demonstrated:

Specific areas that need improvement:

On a scale from 1 to 5, rate the practicum student in relation to this specific learning objective where 1 means "complete failure" and 5 means "complete success." Student Rating: _____

What specific tasks and/or behaviors need to be demonstrated to raise the above rating on the next practicum evaluation? Explain in detail below:

3.16 Other_____

How demonstrated:

How not demonstrated:

Specific areas that need improvement:

On a scale from 1 to 5, rate the practicum student in relation to this specific learning objective where 1 means "complete failure" and 5 means "complete success." Student Rating: _____

What specific tasks and/or behaviors need to be demonstrated to raise the above rating on the next practicum evaluation? Explain in detail below:

LEARNING GOAL 4:
FUNCTIONS EFFECTIVELY WITHIN
AN EVALUATIVE CONTEXT

The student will contribute to the improvement of service delivery by evaluating professional development, effectiveness as a social work practitioner, and the practicum setting.

Learning Objectives

4.1 Has demonstrated the ability to evaluate accurately a level of competence and effectiveness in practice.

How demonstrated:

How not demonstrated:

Specific areas that need improvement:

On a scale from 1 to 5, rate the practicum student in relation to this specific learning objective where 1 means "complete failure" and 5 means "complete success." Student Rating: _____

What specific tasks and/or behaviors need to be demonstrated to raise the above rating on the next practicum evaluation? Explain in detail below:

4.2 Has demonstrated the ability to receive, understand, and consider feedback.

How demonstrated:

How not demonstrated:

Specific areas that need improvement:

On a scale from 1 to 5, rate the practicum student in relation to this specific learning objective where 1 means "complete failure" and 5 means "complete success." Student Rating: _____

What specific tasks and/or behaviors need to be demonstrated to raise the above rating on the next practicum evaluation? Explain in detail below:

4.3 Has demonstrated the ability to evaluate the practicum experience.

How demonstrated:

How not demonstrated:

Specific areas that need improvement:

On a scale from 1 to 5, rate the practicum student in relation to this specific learning objective where 1 means "complete failure" and 5 means "complete success." Student Rating: _____

What specific tasks and/or behaviors need to be demonstrated to raise the above rating on the next practicum evaluation? Explain in detail below:

4.4 Other_____

How demonstrated:

How not demonstrated:

Specific areas that need improvement:

On a scale from 1 to 5, rate the practicum student in relation to this specific learning objective where 1 means "complete failure" and 5 means "complete success." Student Rating: _____

What specific tasks and/or behaviors need to be demonstrated to raise the above rating on the next practicum evaluation? Explain in detail below:

GRADE RECOMMENDED OR ASSESSMENT:

Summary comments by *practicum student*—include areas of strength, any concerns, and focus for continued learning:

Summary comments by *practicum instructor*—include areas of strength, any concerns, and focus for continued learning:

Summary comments by *practicum liaison*—include areas of strength, any concerns, and focus for continued learning:

Signatures:

Student_____

Practicum Instructor_____

Practicum Liaison_____

The Social Work Practicum: An Access Guide
Second Edition

Composition and internal design by Andrukow Compositors,
Calgary, Alberta, Canada

Cover design by Sarah Peacock

Printing and binding by McNaughton & Gunn,
Saline, Michigan

Paper, Publishers Smooth